CHILDREN OF THE MOON

ALSO BY THEODORA LAU

The Chinese Horoscopes Guide to Relationships
The Handbook of Chinese Horoscopes, Fourth Edition
Best-Loved Chinese Proverbs

CHILDREN OF THE MOON

Discover Your Child's Personality
Through Chinese Horoscopes

THEODORA LAU

Chinese Calligraphy by Kenneth Lau
Drawings and Illustrations by Michele Fujimoto

Quill
A HarperResource Book
An Imprint of HarperCollinsPublishers

FIRST EDITION

DESIGNED BY MARY AUSTIN SPEAKER

Library of Congress Cataloging-in-Publication Data
    Lau, Theodora.
        Children of the moon: discover your child's personality through Chinese
        horoscopes /Theodora Lau; Chinese calligraphy by Kenneth Lau;
        drawings & illustrations by Michele Fujimoto.—1st ed.
        p. cm.
    Includes index.
ISBN 0-06-093836-6
1. Astrology, Chinese. 2. Children—Miscellanea. I. Title.

BF1714.C5 L365 2002
133.5'9251—dc21

                                        2002020802

    02 03 04 05 06 ❖RRD 10 9 8 7 6 5 4 3 2 1

CONTENTS

vi

C O N T E N T S

vii

C
O
N
T
E
N
T
S

CONTENTS

CHINESE ASTROLOGY

Children of the Moon

She shines above us like a beacon of love,
Her guidance ever present in the seasons and tides.
We need not shield our eyes from her lovely light
As we must from the glaring sun.

Her radiant beauty holds us forever in awe,
Enthralling us with her many moods, soothing us,
Intriguing us with a multitude of transformations.
Yet, through millennia we seek to understand her mysteries
For we are her children and know
She is our loving patroness.

Mother Moon is the great influence on all growth around us.
We sow and reap by her nurturing hand.
And count the days
and journey by her reckoning in the heavens
Which have never forsaken us.

She knows us all as Earth Branches of the Tree of Life.
And though the branches are many, the root is One.
Reaching out in unison, upward and outward,
We grow under the benevolent auspices of Mother Moon.

INTRODUCTION

TWENTY-TWO YEARS AGO, WHEN I FIRST WROTE *The Handbook of Chinese Horoscopes*, Chinese astrology was viewed as a rather unknown and disorganized subject. My publishers at that time, Harper & Row (now HarperCollins Publishers) did advance research and found that there were only two other books in English on this particularly intriguing subject, but both these books were very basic and did not present an in-depth picture of the fascinating and multifaceted world of Chinese astrology. One book was very superficial and had "fortune cookie"-like sayings that did nothing more than pique one's curiosity without providing any real answers. The other book was based on the Vietnamese version of Chinese horoscopes, which had the Cat in place of the Rabbit as the fourth lunar sign. Both books had many discrepancies and inaccuracies that were detrimental to real Chinese horoscopes as a whole.

Armed with solid research and reliable data, my publishers challenged me to write a book that would address all the questions and explore the different areas that a serious reader would be interested in. From this humble beginning, we crafted a handbook that has "withstood the test of time," and in the year 2000, HarperCollins published the fourth edition of *The Handbook*, which also marked the twentieth anniversary of the work itself. *The Handbook of Chinese Horoscopes* was the first to describe the five elements and how they could be combined with the twelve lunar signs. I created sixty personalities, which have now become an intrinsic part of Chinese horoscope reading. These sixty personalities, now comfortably known by names such as the "Fire Tiger," "Water Dragon," "Wood Monkey," "Metal Snake," and "Earth Boar," were based on friends and family of mine who happened to be born in those particular years and whose traits I wove into each description to bring these characters to life. These combinations and personalities did not exist in any Chinese history or text on this subject before they were created in 1979. Added to that, I created the 144 marriage combinations for the twelve animal signs of the Chinese zodiac and also wrote a special section called: "When Moon Signs Meet Sun Signs." This section of 144 combinations showed the similarities and links between the lunar and solar astrological systems. Again, they were created to have the personality traits of real people.

In the winter of 2000, when I approached my publishers with the idea of doing a book of Chinese horoscopes dedicated to children, Hugh van Dusen, vice president and executive editor of HarperPerennial Books, asked why such a book would be successful. Hugh van Dusen, by the way, was the person over two decades ago who first recognized the potential and popularity of Chinese horoscopes and decided to publish the work of an unknown author from Hong Kong. I have always valued his advice and guidance, and it took me a week of introspection to give him a worthy reply.

My purpose for writing this book is actually threefold. First, I really did feel that children should be looked at through a different light. I told Hugh that through the years many parents, parents-to-be, and grandparents have sought answers and advice on how the personality of their child would be influenced by Chinese astrology. My handbook was written for adults who had already

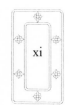

developed their personalities and it focused on relationships and compatibility issues, which were areas that we as adults could understand or remedy on our own. I also had a small section for each of the twelve signs, entitled "the ___ Child," for each one of the twelve animals, and this proved very popular and accurate according to the feedback from my readers.

The first purpose of *Children of the Moon* is to focus on understanding the yet undeveloped personality and potential of each child. It is a profound honor, joy, and responsibility to nurture and raise a child, and it is my hope that Chinese horoscopes will provide new insights into such an important undertaking. Once we are able to understand and appreciate a child's personality, it becomes much easier to guide and work with that particular child in the light of walking with him or her along the same path. We are also better equipped to explain to the child why he or she is different from others, including his or her siblings, and why these differences are a plus and something to be celebrated. I believe that every child looks into the eyes of his or her parent or guardian and sees the image of how he or she is perceived in the mind of the adult. If the child sees disappointment, doubt, confusion, anger, disdain, despair, or any of these negative emotions, the child's self-image will reflect the same values. It is amazing how well a child can read a parent's body language, and how he or she can sense the subtle nuances of communication. We must strive to instill confidence and, more importantly, a positive self-image in every child from birth. He or she should like and believe in himself or herself because the people he or she loves most show that they understand and appreciate this child and all his or her special traits and distinct personality.

The second reason or purpose of writing this book came quite by accident. A lady who read *The Handbook of Chinese Horoscopes* when it was first published in 1979 wrote me a four-page letter and faxed it to me. I was very touched and humbled by her sincere and heartwarming words. We then talked and felt like we had known each other for years, twenty years to be exact, through Chinese horoscopes. I have asked this lady, Linda LaZar, to write her own story as a part of this introduction so that readers could see how Chinese horoscopes worked for children through her valuable life experience. Before hearing from Linda LaZar, I did not know anyone, apart from myself, who actually utilized my interpretations of Chinese horoscopes in such a practical way to give guidance to their children.

The third reason and purpose for writing this book is because the last of my three children, Laura, had just graduated from the University of California, Berkeley, or "Cal," as they call it for short, and she reminisced about how she grew up with Chinese horoscopes and how it affected and shaped her views on life. I was not able to dedicate my first book to Laura, as she was not yet born at that time, so I was pleasantly surprised when she offered to write a short essay, titled "The Failure List," for this book. As a "child of the moon," or of lunar horoscopes, I hope Laura's firsthand experiences will provide readers with some form of enlightenment of how the influence of Chinese horoscopes made an impression on a young person's life.

In all my previous four editions of *The Handbook of Chinese Horoscopes* and also in my second book, *The Chinese Horoscopes Guide to Relationships*, I delved into marriages, compatibility, affinity triangles, conflict, and 144 different combination personalities when Eastern horoscopes merge with your Western sign, such as the Aries Rat, Taurean Ox, Libran Tiger, Leo Dragon, and so forth. Please feel free to refer to these two other books to gain the basic insight and foundation needed to appreciate Chinese horoscopes, as I will not dwell too much on similar subjects here, but rather concentrate on the early development and traits of each child that are easily discernible through Chinese horoscopes. I will emphasize on the ascendant of the child, his or her basic nature, and possible relationships with parents and siblings. I will touch on the general outlook that each child may develop, and also discuss to a lesser degree how the birth order affects each lunar sign differently. Knowing the strengths and limitations of each child and showing that you will stand behind that child through thick or thin is already ensuring that half the battle is won. The other half should be a happy alliance that parents and child can share in, and they should grow together through the valuable journey of bonding. Because the most precious gift we could ever give a child is the gift of our time.

As always, here is reaching out to one and all in harmony and understanding. Happy reading!

—*Theodora Lau*

A NOTE ON THE TWELVE CHILDREN'S STORIES IN THIS BOOK

THE TWELVE CHILDREN'S STORIES IN THIS BOOK were originally created by the author as part of a collection of new Chinese fables published under a separate title. While some of them do have roots in old Chinese stories, their endings have been modified to give youngsters a positive image with which to identify. Each story is crafted to provide a special message and to reflect the best traits of each lunar sign in Chinese astrology. It is the author's hope that emphasizing the nobler aspects of each character's intrinsic nature will help increase a child's understanding and pride in his or her own personality.

The author spent considerable time researching Chinese as well as other Asian children's stories and was appalled and disappointed at the violence (Rat losing its tail), undertones of aggression (Dragons bullying others), lack of fair play (Monkey taking unfair advantage), and absence of moral values wherein might makes right and the victim does not get justice. She also had difficulty finding the appropriate happy endings that could impart the lessons and lasting impressions that she felt needed to be conveyed to our children. Hence, she wove her own stories with upbeat, happy endings in which each of the twelve main animal characters are able to resolve important issues and handle problems in wise, fair, responsible, and peaceful ways. Each is able to become a hero or heroine through his or her own unique traits and resourcefulness.

In this book, the author stresses the higher qualities of human nature by giving animals human traits and personalities. For instance, in the Tiger's story, we learn that kindness is just as important as intelligence. In the Rooster's story, we learn that friends can share or trade their gifts or talents, finding both success and happiness. In the Rat's story, we find that size does not matter. Intelligence is more valuable than sheer size or physical strength.

The author wishes to stress that no one lunar sign is stronger or better than another, they are all equal and original in their own right. It is up to us to uncover and develop the positive and better side of our nature and to celebrate our many intrinsic strengths and wonderful talents.

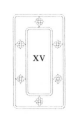

PARENTING WITH CHINESE HOROSCOPES

BY LINDA LAZAR

Y OU ARE ABOUT TO READ ONE OF THE MOST wonderful guides to parenting that you will ever encounter. Theodora Lau has been my mentor in the science of Chinese astrology for over twenty years. It was her first book, *Handbook of Chinese Horoscopes*, which I purchased in 1979, that inspired me to begin my amazing journey into the enlightenment of the human personality.

There are hundreds of books available to teach parents everything from diaper changing to applying for college scholarships. You can also find psychology books with instructions on how to handle troubled children. That's great, but wouldn't it be better if you could avoid having a troubled child in the first place?

Psychology and Western medicine are very useful as post-problem remedies. But Eastern philosophy encourages prevention through understanding in every arena of life—health, career, and relationships. Chinese astrology takes this approach one step further. It not only helps us prevent potential problems, it identifies and encourages our strengths and potential areas of success. This is the key.

I have utilized my knowledge of Chinese astrology to raise my children. During my pregnancies, I studied their signs; I began to understand their personalities before they were even born. They are both incredible people, with tremendous potential. Because of this approach, I understand their potential, their natural strengths and weaknesses. I have been able to direct them away from dwelling upon their weaknesses by encouraging them to focus upon their strengths. I believe that because of parenting based upon Theodora Lau's approach to astrology, my two children both became honor students who are well behaved, self-motivated, ambitious, and good-natured.

Over the years, using the knowledge originally inspired by Theodora's work, I was able to summon up the courage to write dozens of newspaper articles and hundreds of radio programs answering questions about how to help children. I know from experience that there is a great need for the book you are about to read. Parents all over the world face the same sorts of situations. For instance, I received a letter from a reader who had concerns and frustrations about her two children and their challenging personalities. She was at wits' end with their behavior, and she wondered if she was somehow guilty of providing a bad environment or poor parenting skills. Her Gemini/Tiger son seemed extremely energetic and talkative, and her Leo/Dragon daughter, who was demanding and willful, gave her grief with their diverse and powerful personalities.

With the assurance that her children's personalities were consistent with their astrological birth signs, and suggestions and guidance toward working with their personalities rather than discouraging them, she felt empowered. When I offered her an analogy that her children's personalities were like flowing rivers—if guided toward outlets they could accomplish positive results, but stopping the natural flow could result in unhappiness, bottled-up hostilities, and perhaps even disaster—she had a different perspective as well as new hope.

It is important to understand, also, that only a woman with extreme fortitude could endure the unlimited demands that go with parenting two such powerful children. She should be proud of herself for providing an environment where her children were able to express themselves naturally. Parents need reassurance and guidance that they are on the right paths.

Chinese astrology offers assistance by suggesting ways of channeling energy and using it constructively. I believe, for instance, the Gemini/Tiger child could succeed where others would fail from their lack of endurance. This type of sign should be encouraged to use his natural instincts where they would best serve him, such as in situations where public speaking, energy, and wit is an advantage rather than a disadvantage. And a Leo/Dragon's powerful and commanding personality should truly be considered an asset, not a personality flaw. It's not just anyone who can enter a room and take command.

If parents could know the natural strengths and weaknesses of their children from the moment they are born, they would be able to encourage and direct their children toward their strengths and explain their weaker aspects. Weakness is not bad, it can actually prove to be their greatest asset if understood and appreciated. The key is to know everybody naturally has them, but one must be productive and work at turning it around to serve one's best interests. Weaknesses should never make us unproductive but be approached as opportunities and converted into strength.

I honor Theodora Lau's role in the evolution of the art of astrology. This Chinese science has enabled us to use the moon to enlighten and to guide us. The science helps us work with the influence of the moon. It saves us from wasting our precious time trying to change that which cannot be changed. Instead of lamenting our differences or criticizing the shortcomings of others, it helps us understand and have tolerance for others.

I personally feel that I have accomplished so much more with my life and those of my children because I understand how to work with the tools we have

been born with. Theodora Lau is sharing the ancient science and her incredible understanding of it with us in a simple, informative, and direct way. I feel very fortunate to have her work available to inspire me and provide focused direction and practical support in my role as a parent for these last two decades.

THE FAILURE LIST

BY LAURA LAU

U PON GRADUATING FROM COLLEGE, my mother (the author of this book) asked me to answer the question: "What makes a good parent?" A loaded question, indeed, but since recent college graduates are experts in reflection, I thought I'd have a go at thinking about all the things that my parents did right in raising me.

By nature, I am a pack rat. I keep anything and everything I think has some value, which means most everything. This meant that moving away from my nesting place of college life necessitated some serious cleaning. I painfully had to throw away every treasured piece of paper, everything, that is, except for my correspondence. Over the years, I wrote to my parents and friends and received and collected an impressive amount of letters and notes, most importantly my mother's. I spoke to my parents on the phone at least once a week, rain or shine, while I was away. Even still, my mother sent me notes and cards to keep my spirits up or to keep me focused upon my goals and assignments.

When I was growing up, my mother used to cut out articles from magazines and collect newspaper clippings, such as Dear Abby or Ann Landers columns, and stuck them onto my bathroom mirror so that I could read them while I brushed my teeth and got ready for school. She told me that this way, I could not run away from her advice. I have to admit that I found the reminders pretty annoying, especially in the morning when I was in a hurry and in no mood to go to school, let alone be lectured. It only made sense that these notes followed me into college. The funny thing is that after years of seeing those notes in front of me, I found myself tacking up the clippings I received onto my own apartment mirror. Apparently, one can never fight the power of conditioning. Here is the list that motivated me to graduate from UC Berkeley while keeping up dental hygiene for four years:

The Failure List

- Einstein was four years old before he could speak.

- Isaac Newton did poorly in grade school and was considered "unpromising."

- Beethoven's music teacher once said of him, "As a composer, he is hopeless."

- When Thomas Edison was a youngster, his teacher told him he was too stupid to learn anything. He was counseled to go into a field where he might succeed by virtue of his pleasant personality.

- F. W. Woolworth got a job in a dry-goods store when he was twenty-one, but his employer would not permit him to wait on customers because he "didn't have enough sense to close a sale."

- Michael Jordan was cut from his high school basketball team. Boston Celtics Hall of Famer Bob Cousy suffered the same fate.

- A newspaper editor fired Walt Disney because he "lacked imagination and had no good ideas."

- Winston Churchill failed the sixth grade and had to repeat it because he did not complete the tests that were required for promotion.

- Babe Ruth struck out 1,300 times—a major-league record.

- Jack Welch was made fun of as a youngster because he stuttered. But, his mother convinced him that it was because his mind was going faster than his tongue and that eventually his tongue would catch up with his mind and the stuttering would stop. It did.

- A person may make mistakes but isn't a failure until he or she starts blaming someone else. We must believe in ourselves, and somewhere along the road of life, we meet someone who sees greatness in us, expects it from us, and lets us know it. It is the golden key to success.

What my mother did right for not only me but also my brother and sister, is that she knew how different we all are. In never letting us give up, she too never gave up in retooling her communication with us. Growing up as the youngest child, I would often make comparisons, measuring my success and progress according to where my brother and sister were at my age. This rarely ever encouraged me; instead I was left to wallow in the differences I imagined. Many of the slips of paper that my mother sent me often took issue with this. Asserting my new independence away from home, I would often fold them up and let them stack up on my desk.

But, as I said before, I always keep things that I feel are valuable to me. I could never rationalize throwing away anything that my mother felt was important enough to send me. I figured the message must be worthwhile, so I kept it, and you know, anytime that I was down and needed some advice, I con-sulted those sheets of paper. Some reminded me of my good points, while others pointed out places where I could improve. Of course, while these bits of criticism were no after-dinner treats, I still gave them the same amount of attention as the compliments.

Now, at the ripe old age of twenty-one, I begin to see that parents need to understand how each child listens and learns. Mine understood that with me it takes constant vigilance in the form of a never-ending stream of little notes of paper. Like every message, with the correct strategy, it eventually sinks in. As children grow, they teach their parents a great deal, too. They grow into their own person, and while a child never truly becomes a peer, the gap in age does decrease. Being a parent is not just the exchange of consolation and advice but a constant assessment of who your child is and who he or she will become when nurtured to full potential. This should never be pushing a child toward what the parent wishes, but encouragement to find where he or she belongs. Along the way, we all learn to listen better and talk a bit less, but most importantly, we don't believe in failure. As an old Chinese proverb says: "Fall nine times—Get up ten," or in other, more familiar words: "Failure is the Mother of Success."*

*Taken from "Best-Loved Chinese Proverbs" by Theodora Lau. My mother wrote this proverb book because she said that all parents like to have the last word and any adage that begins with "Old Chinese Saying" is always effective to quell arguments, especially from children.

THE LUNAR YEARS FROM 1984 TO 2019
(Three Cycles of Twelve Years)

The Start and End Dates Are from the Western/Solar Calendar*

YEAR	LUNAR SIGN	START DATE		END DATE	ELEMENT OF THE YEAR
1984	Rat	February 2, 1984	to	January 19, 1985	Wood
1985	Ox	February 20, 1985	to	February 8, 1986	Wood
1986	Tiger	February 9, 1986	to	January 28, 1987	Fire
1987	Rabbit	January 29, 1987	to	February 16, 1988	Fire
1988	Dragon	February 17, 1988	to	February 5, 1989	Earth
1989	Snake	February 6, 1989	to	January 26, 1990	Earth
1990	Horse	January 27, 1990	to	February 14, 1991	Metal
1991	Sheep	February 15, 1991	to	February 3, 1992	Metal
1992	Monkey	February 4, 1992	to	January 22, 1993	Water
1993	Rooster	January 23, 1993	to	February 9, 1994	Water
1994	Dog	February 10, 1994	to	January 30, 1995	Wood
1995	Boar	January 31, 1995	to	February 18, 1996	Wood
1996	Rat	January 19, 1996	to	February 6, 1997	Fire
1997	Ox	February 7, 1997	to	January 27, 1998	Fire
1998	Tiger	January 28, 1998	to	February 15, 1999	Earth
1999	Rabbit	February 16, 1999	to	February 4, 2000	Earth
2000	Dragon	February 5, 2000	to	January 23, 2001	Metal
2001	Snake	January 24, 2001	to	February 11, 2002	Metal
2002	Horse	February 12, 2002	to	January 31, 2003	Water
2003	Sheep	February 1, 2003	to	January 21, 2004	Water
2004	Monkey	January 22, 2004	to	February 8, 2005	Wood
2005	Rooster	February 9, 2005	to	January 28, 2006	Wood
2006	Dog	January 29, 2006	to	February 17, 2007	Fire
2007	Boar	February 18, 2007	to	February 6, 2008	Fire
2008	Rat	February 7, 2008	to	January 25, 2009	Earth
2009	Ox	January 26, 2009	to	February 13, 2010	Earth

YEAR	LUNAR SIGN	START DATE		END DATE	ELEMENT OF THE YEAR
2010	Tiger	February 14, 2010	to	February 2, 2011	Metal
2011	Rabbit	February 3, 2011	to	January 22, 2012	Metal
2012	Dragon	January 23, 2012	to	February 9, 2013	Water
2013	Snake	February 10, 2013	to	January 30, 2014	Water
2014	Horse	January 31, 2014	to	February 18, 2015	Wood
2015	Sheep	February 19, 2015	to	February 7, 2016	Wood
2016	Monkey	February 8, 2016	to	January 27, 2017	Fire
2017	Rooster	January 28, 2017	to	February 15, 2018	Fire
2018	Dog	February 16, 2018	to	February 4, 2019	Earth
2019	Boar	February 5, 2019	to	January 24, 2020	Earth

* Year text for conversion dates are taken from the Ten Thousand Years (Perpetual) Chinese Calendar. The twenty-first century begins at the cusp of the Dragon and Snake years. Please check the exact dates according to the start and end dates on this chart, as lunar years overlap in the Western calendar.

A NOTE FROM THE AUTHOR ABOUT PRONOUNS AND GENDER

IN CHINESE HOROSCOPES, THERE ARE SIX yang signs that are also known as positive, active, or masculine signs. They are the Rat, the Tiger, the Dragon, the Horse, the Monkey, and the Dog. In ranking order, they are the odd numbers: one, three, five, seven, nine, and eleven in the Chinese zodiac. Male pronouns are used in the six chapters dealing with these signs.

For the Six yin, or feminine animal, signs: the Ox, the Rabbit, the Snake, the Sheep, the Rooster, and the Boar, the female pronouns are used in the corresponding chapters—two, four, six, eight, ten, and twelve.

The alternative use of male and female pronouns to match the yang and yin stems of each lunar sign is the easiest and most impartial way to have only one pronoun per chapter and maintain equality between the sexes. Needless to say, the female pronouns apply equally to every male child born under a yin sign and vice versa for females born under yang signs.

CHAPTER ONE

THE RAT

The First Lunar Sign

The Rat is a self-starter.

Even as a link he manages to function as a complete unit.

Innovative and intelligent,

A native of this first sign is

A born leader and problem solver.

Life is one continuous journey of discovery,

Each search ends with a new quest and challenge.

The Rat sign signifies progress, exploration, and deep insight.

He excels in communications and teamwork.

His motto is: **ALL FOR ONE AND ONE FOR ALL!**

THE RAT'S BRANCH

CHINESE NAME FOR THE RAT: *Shu*

RANK: First

HOURS OF THE RAT: From 11 P.M. to 12:59 A.M.*

DIRECTION OF THIS BRANCH: North

SEASON AND PRINCIPAL MONTH: Winter and December

CORRESPONDS TO THE WESTERN SIGN: Sagittarius, the Archer

FIXED ELEMENT: Water

STEM: Yang, or masculine

* Ascendant: *Children who are born during the two-hour segment of the day ruled by the Rat sign will have this sign as their ascendant and will display affinity for people born under this particular sign, as well as have many of the distinct character traits that identify the Rat sign.*

FIVE CYCLES* OF THE LUNAR YEARS OF THE RAT IN THE WESTERN CALENDAR

START DATE		END DATE	ELEMENT OF THE YEAR
January 28, 1960	to	February 14, 1961	Metal
February 16, 1972	to	February 2, 1973	Water
February 2, 1984	to	February 19, 1985	Wood
January 19, 1996	to	February 6, 1997	Fire
February 7, 2008	to	January 25, 2009	Earth

* A cycle on the lunar horoscope equals twelve years. Five cycles completes sixty years.

Note: One who is born on the day before the start of the lunar year of the Rat, e.g., January 27, 1960, will belong to the animal sign before the Rat, which is the Boar, the twelfth lunar sign. One who is born on the day after the end of the lunar year of the Rat, e.g., February 15, 1961, will belong to the animal sign following the Rat, which is the Ox, the second lunar sign.

鼠

我為人人人為我

克昌題 美秀畫

THE RAT SIGN
ALL FOR ONE AND ONE FOR ALL

The Rat Personality

The first earth branch of the Chinese lunar cycle is named *Zi* and is symbolized by the Rat. This is the sign of the initiator who loves to be involved and actively participating in everything that goes around him. The *Zi* personality is a doer and a leader. He is unusually alert, inquisitive, and intelligent. A child born in the year of the first earth branch needs a lot of attention and love. In return, he will be extremely affectionate and responsive. Outwardly, he may appear shy and quiet, but in reality his *Zi* personality is competitive and fiercely possessive of his loved ones, especially his mother. This closeness will remain throughout his life, if the child is able to bond properly. *Zi* personalities usually have no problem bonding with their parents. Because of their innate need for security and love, many children of the first earth branch tend to cling to people or caregivers they identify with and take separation very hard. He has a fear of abandonment and does not like being left alone for any period of time. The first day of school, a new baby-sitter, a new home, any change of environment affects Rat children especially hard. But, once they have overcome their fears and get into the hang of things, they are sociable and make friends easily.

In spite of his charming and sweet disposition, the Rat child does resort to crying and whining to get his way and will learn to talk early, as communication skills are vital to him. This is just as well, as this personality is good at expressing himself and is never in doubt about what he likes and dislikes. As a parent, it will be easy to know how to please this baby or child, since there is no guesswork to be done. If you observe a Rat baby carefully, you will note that even before he learns to speak, he will be able to use his hands or even his eyes to sign and communicate what he wants from you. The main job is to constantly reassure this child that he has your full support and love no matter what happens. Your unconditional love is something that he will need to carry throughout life and will become his touchstone in times of trouble and uncertainty.

Children of the first branch tend to love eating and enjoy different tastes and textures of food at an early age. Later, they do take an active interest in cooking and will find their way around in the kitchen, helping with chores and with younger siblings. Easy to teach and quick to learn, children of this first branch are usually delightful to have around the house. If he is the talkative type, he could liven up any party or play group with banter and bossiness that is warm and quite entertaining.

This child will be able to keep track of his belongings and will develop an early urge to be a collector. As he grows, he may become more possessive and acquisitive, and although he may not be the most tidy or organized child, he will certainly have an excellent memory of what is his and a mental inventory of his toys. He is very sentimental. Don't try to get rid of anything without telling him or he will develop a mistrust for others taking his stuff when he is not around, and that will just magnify his innate need to horde and accumulate. This even extends to storing all kinds of food, snacks, and drinks in his room. Yet, even if he does have a suspicious side to his nature, he will always be generous, forgiving, and affectionate to his loved ones, especially his parents.

It is considered a blessing in the East to have a child born in the Rat year, as he will always be around to look after his parents when they grow old. In the eyes of the Rat, or *Zi*, personality, his parents and loved ones can do no wrong. He will cater to their needs and overlook any shortcomings because in the nest of the family, the Rat child finds true happiness.

The hardworking, vivacious *Zi* child will love to read and learn how to write early. Given the necessary encouragement, he will be ambitious and very creative. Children of the first earth branch take to music, drawing, singing, and have a multitude of talent because they are not afraid to try their hand at anything they find interesting. So, if the parents are musically inclined, this child will observe his parents and will be mimicking them and catch on in no time. The Rat child makes friends easily because he loves group activity and is able to communicate and participate without being difficult or stubborn. He will show his resourcefulness early in life and can be quite assertive if he thinks he is being shortchanged in any way. A child of this earth branch can become critical, argumentative, and crafty when he is thwarted by unfair or oppressive rules. He is a willing and hard worker but may love to bargain or haggle for every little thing, such as moving his bedtime, watching ten more minutes of television, or having another cookie. It is quite useless to be angry with him or to punish him. Remember, these same negotiating skills will get him far in life, and whatever he earns, whatever good deals he can get, and gains from his business or career later in life will always go to his own family first. It is far better to have him on your side.

The Rat child is quick to sense any underlying tension and nuances and will know immediately when someone is upset or angry with him. His natural intuition teaches him early in life to assess situations, which adults may think him incapable of doing. Do not underestimate his sharpness and ability to feel the hidden pulse of what is actually going on around him. He may not know how to pretend, because of his innocence, but you will certainly know he senses that something is afoot by his astute questions. More often than not, he is right.

Birth Order and Sibling Rivalry

*FIRSTBORN OR ONLY CHILD

When the Rat child is the firstborn or only child, he will be a natural leader. But, his leadership will be by consensus and not at all dictatorial. He is thoughtful of his parents and siblings and would never go things alone without consulting with them. This is because he learns to communicate well and could explain to others why and how things should be done his way. Of course, not everyone will agree with him, but then his charm and ability to get others to cooperate is quite legendary, and in the end, he is able to sell his ideas and get the support he needs. The Rat child is talkative and competitive. A natural scholar and writer, he will excel in school and be active in all sorts of extracurricular activities. He always wants to be part of the team even if he is not the

---

* When a child is born five years after another child, he or she is also considered a firstborn child.

leader; he always has something important to contribute. If he is the firstborn or only child, he is able to take center stage and receive the full attention of his parents without any competition. He loves this. In return, he will idolize his parents and follow them everywhere. Possessive and inquisitive, he will want to do everything his parents do. If they are in the medical profession, he will pretend he is a doctor or nurse and carry a little stethoscope; if they play golf, he will want his own miniature set; if they play a musical instrument, he will play it, too. The wonderful thing about this child is that he is easy to teach and influence. He rarely questions authority. He tends to glorify his parents and feels very close to one or both parents. The Rat as firstborn is kind and nurturing to younger siblings. He really enjoys their company and will always have a protective arm around his brothers and sisters. The main problem this child will have is that he strives to do too much and is easily stressed when the responsibilities become too heavy.

MIDDLE OR LATER-BORN CHILD

The Rat as the middle child will be more assertive and competitive because he has to vie for attention from the firstborn. He works hard to earn affection. The only one who could work harder for attention is a twin of the firstborn. The Rat as the middle child could feel that he is shortchanged and has to copy his older sibling and his parents as role models. In trying to excel and displace the first born, the Rat child in the middle position is always attentive to his parents' wishes and tries to be on par with the firstborn or even to get one notch higher. He is able to take responsibility and tends to be domineering when he is in charge. In order to upgrade himself, he is often jealous of the firstborn and will want to have everything his older sibling has or even more. Throughout life, he tends to need reassurance that he is the best and equal to the older sibling, if not better than the firstborn. The middle child or later born is very people oriented and will be popular at school. This child is also kind, generous, and helpful to younger siblings, who pose no threat, and likes the role of authority when the parents or teacher leaves him in charge. The Rat child as the middle or later

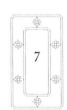

born is most in need of mentoring and should be made to feel special. If he has a special talent, such as the ability to sing or draw, he should be encouraged to develop his gift without any interference from the firstborn.

YOUNGEST OR LAST-BORN CHILD

The youngest is defined as the younger of two children or the youngest of all the siblings. This is a nice niche for the Rat child born in this position. He will be spoiled by the parents and all the older siblings because of his sweet and charming disposition. Of course, he will whine and cling and do all sorts of antics to stay at the center of attention. Yet, they will all cater to him because of his loving and engaging personality. Talkative, helpful, cooperative, and affectionate, the Rat child as the youngest is loved and doted on by the whole family. No doubt, he will use his position as the baby to the fullest extent. He is clever and crafty and will always know how to maneuver himself into the good graces of his parents, teachers, and siblings. As the youngest, this child expects others to do things for him and could be quite complacent and lazy if not held to higher standards. He must be prodded to work hard and be more competitive.

Ascendants

In Chinese horoscopes, the two-hour segment ruling the time of birth is known as the ascendant sign. This can also be referred to as the child's "inner self."

The time of birth used to determine the ascendant is always the local time in the place of birth.

For a child born in the Year of the Rat:

THE RAT ASCENDANT—TIME OF BIRTH IS BETWEEN 11 P.M. AND 12:59 A.M.
This child is bound to be very charming and intuitive but also self-absorbed. Openly inquisitive and curious, he loves to be the center of attention. With this

ascendant, the Rat child is quick to learn new things, and is agile and mentally superior. On the other hand, he could also be demanding and impatient. This child can also be very possessive and intent on having his way. Quick to learn the value of the spoken and written word, this child has no problem communicating his wishes clearly. You will probably get a detailed list of what he wants the minute this child learns to write, and he will learn very early!

THE OX ASCENDANT—TIME OF BIRTH IS BETWEEN 1 A.M. AND 2:59 A.M.
This child will still have the Rat's engaging and appealing qualities, but he will have a more serious nature and favors the quiet, discipline ways of the Ox. The influence of this ascendant is a strong sense of duty and responsibility. Though he will favor stability and comfort, this does not mean this Rat will not have the same sense of adventure as his brothers and sisters. He will be motivated to meet his goals, with the Ox's steadfast nature combined with that of the intuitive Rat. Hardworking and efficient, a child with this ascendant follows through and is dependable. On the other hand, he may also be a bit of a taskmaster and expects others to follow all the rules and keep their promises.

THE TIGER ASCENDANT—TIME OF BIRTH IS BETWEEN 3 A.M. AND 4:59 A.M.
This child is destined to be colorful, strong, and confident. The Tiger's fiery qualities ensure that this Rat will excel at most anything he is determined to do. He will hate remaining still, choosing a life of constant motion and escapades that could test his parents' patience. As a result of the Tiger ascendant, this child could be impulsive in his actions yet very unselfish and generous with gifts and favors; therefore, the lesson of moderation must be instilled early. The outgoing Tiger within instills a love of excitement that complements a show-stopping personality and a natural talent for entertaining.

THE RABBIT ASCENDANT—TIME OF BIRTH IS BETWEEN 5 A.M. AND 6:59 A.M.
This combination of Rabbit and Rat produces a child with grace and level-headed action. He has a cool and collected attitude, ideal for mediation and problem solving. Sociable yet practical and calm, this child minds his manners

and can also be polite and reasonable, especially when he is negotiating to get his way. A charming diplomat, this child can achieve greatness with the Rabbit's winning personality and the Rat's ambition and insight.

THE DRAGON ASCENDANT—TIME OF BIRTH IS BETWEEN 7 A.M. AND 8:59 A.M.

The Dragon ascendant produces a child with a sincere heart, fearless love, and selfless generosity. This child is very outgoing and will have many friends and followers, but must guard against people taking advantage of his benevolent personality. Fortunately, the Rat side has a cautionary nature and tends to be more calculating and suspicious than the magnanimous Dragon. This child will be a natural leader, loving the limelight but also able to handle the responsibility that comes with it. The Rat and Dragon personalities merge to truly create a magical synergy.

THE SNAKE ASCENDANT—TIME OF BIRTH IS BETWEEN 9 A.M. AND 10:59 A.M.

At times this child will be difficult to figure out, but that's just the way he will like it. In fact, this mystery surrounding this private and creative child with a Snake ascendant will invite many admirers. He will always look before he leaps. The Snake and Rat combination produces an intelligent and thoughtful child who chooses to confide only in family and true friends. Sure of themselves, these children will not be easily influenced and will show independence and wisdom very early in life.

THE HORSE ASCENDANT—TIME OF BIRTH IS BETWEEN 11 A.M. AND 12:59 P.M.

This child will be one of action in every area of life. The Horse ascendant invokes a loving and carefree spirit. As a result, he will seek adventure through travel and relationships. He will love drama, danger, and excitement and tends to take risks that will worry his parents. The passionate nature of the Horse will influence his decisions. This child is open with his feelings and never makes halfhearted commitments. Hopefully, the Rat self will curb the Horse's delight for adventure, knowing when to pull in the reins and when to run free and fast.

THE SHEEP ASCENDANT—TIME OF BIRTH IS BETWEEN 1 P.M. AND 2:59 P.M.

The Sheep gives this young Rat a loving and sensitive nature, but this means that one should be cautious with criticism. He does not take to setbacks well. This is a child that needs to be surrounded by love and support. With good taste and an eye for the finer points in life, he naturally will move to creative outlets to communicate thoughts and emotions. He has a keen understanding of what makes himself and others tick. Beware, he can be very persuasive despite his naturally shy and quiet nature.

THE MONKEY ASCENDANT—TIME OF BIRTH IS BETWEEN 3 P.M. AND 4:59 P.M.

There is no stopping this child with the Monkey and Rat combination. A born strategist, he will come up with ways of approaching a situation that others will not even see. Puzzles and challenging games will fascinate this child, who loves to solve problems and investigate how things work. He will love to entertain and perform with irresistible charm and the ability to improvise. A little chatterbox, the Monkey ascendant never lets this child take no for an answer.

THE ROOSTER ASCENDANT—TIME OF BIRTH IS BETWEEN 5 P.M. AND 6:59 P.M.

The Rooster within this child produces a captivating yet complicated personality—an eye for detail and imagination that produces grand dreams and aspirations. Of course, these wishes are possible with the Rat's outgoing personality and the confidence and perseverance of the tireless Rooster. He may need to learn how to hold his tongue, although the Rat's natural charm could save the day. The Rooster ascendant makes this child a bit of a perfectionist who must do everything right. He tends to fuss when things are not up to his standard, so you can rest assured that he will be a good student and get his homework done ahead of schedule.

THE DOG ASCENDANT—TIME OF BIRTH IS BETWEEN 7 P.M. AND 8:59 P.M.

This child will weigh all sides of a situation before making a decision. The Rat side will opt for the easy way out, but the loyal inner self of the Dog likes to obey all the rules and treat others equally. The Rat's ambition is tempered by the fairness and compassion of the Dog. Still, it does not hurt to instill a good conscience into a child that is naturally opportunistic and aggressive. The Dog personality also makes this child strong-willed and articulate. He or she will never back down from a fight and hates being bullied. On the whole, he does make friends easily and is outgoing. He could channel his competitiveness and his need to excel through sports.

THE BOAR ASCENDANT—TIME OF BIRTH IS BETWEEN 9 P.M. AND 10:59 P.M.
Popularity will naturally find this gracious and big-hearted child. The Boar has a natural sensibility that complements the fun-loving yet clever Rat. He will never be able to act without first considering how every action will affect the other. Thoughtful and caring, his friends and admirers will never be far away. This child will be envied by peers for his wide circle of friends and influence. He has the knack for bringing everyone together and tends to be able to get along with everyone without much trouble. On the other hand, this child also has the tendency to be too good-hearted and naive. He could easily be hurt by the selfishness and greed of others if he does not assert himself early in life.

Famous Persons Born in the Year of the Rat

William Shakespeare
George Sand
Sidney Poitier
Marlon Brando
Pope John Paul I
Wolfgang A. Mozart
Pablo Casals
Gene Kelly
Yves St. Laurent
Leo Tolstoy
Maurice Chevalier
Peggy Fleming
Andrew Lloyd Webber

James Baldwin
Jimmy Carter
Doris Day
James Callaghan
Charlotte Brontë
Karim Aga Khan IV
Lauren Bacall
Thomas Hardy
F. W. de Klerk
Jules Verne
Prince Charles
Al Gore
George H. Bush

As a treat to your child, please read the Rat's story,
"How the Rat Got to Be Number One," which follows.

THE RAT'S STORY

"HOW THE RAT GOT TO BE NUMBER ONE"

When the great Lord Buddha was ready to depart the earth, he entrusted Ms. Rat with the mission to tell all the other animals to come for a final blessing at a special time and place. The efficient Ms. Rat was diligent in getting the good news out. She made sure all the other animals knew the appointed time and place for them to gather and bid the Lord Buddha farewell. The Rat was most energetic and thorough in fulfilling her mission. But, although Ms. Rat told a great many animals about the Buddha's invitation, only twelve, including Ms. Rat, showed up at the Lord Buddha's appointed time and place.

To reward each of these thoughtful animals, the Buddha named each of the twelve earth branches after one of the animals in the order of arrival and also appointed a year to honor that particular animal. Now, there developed a big problem as the Rat and the Ox both claimed to have arrived first. Some of the other animals said that the Rat was first, but others swore that the Ox was earlier. Still others, who were trying to be diplomatic, said they both arrived at the exact same moment. The Lord Buddha did not want to be the one to make the decision. He felt that it was something to be resolved by the animals themselves, since they would have to live with their choice. So the animals discussed among themselves how to choose the one who would be given the honor of being Number One.

"Mr. Ox is big and strong and reliable. He would be a good leader," said the Lady Rabbit, who admired the Ox's strength and character.

"Yes, but at times, Mr. Ox is also stubborn, rigid, and dictatorial," said the gentle Ms. Sheep and her friend the happy Ms. Boar, who were a little afraid of the Ox, and with good reason.

"We must also consider the fact that Ms. Rat was most helpful in delivering the Lord Buddha's invitation to everyone. Ms. Rat worked hard and should be recognized for her efforts," asserted the Dragon, who thought highly of the charming Rat.

"Ah, but Ms. Rat is weak and puny in size and she could be squashed by Mr. Ox, who is powerful and imposing," observed the Tiger and the Horse, who both felt that size was important in selecting a good leader.

Upon hearing that last remark, Ms. Rat jumped up on the podium and declared:

"If I could get all of you to say that a Rat can be bigger than an Ox, would you choose me for the Number One spot?"

"What?? A Rat bigger than an Ox?" laughed all the other animals.

"Yes, we would definitely vote for such a large Rat."

"Then it is agreed," said the wise Lady Snake. "Let us all meet tonight at this stage up against that large temple wall to make a judgment and decide once and for all who will be the first in the lunar cycle." As the other animals left one by one, only two animals stayed behind: the Rat and her dear friend Mr. Monkey, who were deep in conversation, with their heads close together as if they were working on a plan.

At the agreed time, Mr. Ox was, as usual, on time, if not early, to show up on the stage. One by one, the others came and took their places in a circle. Finally, everyone was present except for Ms. Rat and Mr. Monkey. The group waited restlessly for the last two to show up.

"Maybe Ms. Rat decided not to take part in the contest," said the Dog. "If the Rat does not arrive in a few more minutes, we shall have to declare Mr. Ox the winner."

All the others nodded in agreement, for the Dog was always fair and spoke the truth.

Suddenly, they heard Mr. Monkey announce in a loud, dramatic voice as he appeared on the stage:

"My fellow animals, may I present to you, Ms. Rat!"

There against the temple wall was the largest shadow of a Rat they had ever seen. Mr. Monkey held a lantern in front of the Rat, who emerged from a hole in the podium. The light of the lantern projected such a large shadow of Ms. Rat that its size was indeed bigger than the Ox who stood on the stage.

In their collective surprise, all the animals said in one voice:

"Look, Ms. Rat is bigger than Mr. Ox!"

They had spoken the judgment aloud, giving the unanimous vote to Ms. Rat. All the animals realized that what Ms. Rat lacked in size, she made up for in ingenuity, intelligence, and crafty strategy. These were all the qualities of a good and able leader. Ms. Rat had won the right to be named Number One in the cycle.

The Lord Buddha smiled in agreement as he left quietly, because he knew that Ms. Rat had not only gained the recognition and respect that she deserved but had succeeded in showing her wisdom to all the other animals. Leadership and intelligence counted more than size. And that was how the Rat got to be Number One.

17

牛

CHAPTER TWO

THE OX

The Second Lunar Sign

The Ox is a stabilizing force—

Steady, determined, and unhurried,

She takes responsibility seriously and

Gets the job done properly.

In times of adversity, she stands

Resolute and unimpeachable.

Seeking to serve integrity,

She will bear the burdens of righteousness,

Without complaint or animosity.

The Ox weaves her own destiny

Through dedication and hard work.

Her motto is: **ALL THINGS COME TO HIM WHO WAITS**

THE OX'S BRANCH

CHINESE NAME FOR THE OX: *Niú*

RANK: Second

HOURS OF THE OX: From 1 A.M. to 2:59 A.M.*

DIRECTION OF THIS BRANCH: North-northeast

SEASON AND PRINCIPAL MONTH: Winter and January

CORRESPONDS TO THE WESTERN SIGN: Capricorn, the Mountain Goat

FIXED ELEMENT: Water

STEM: Yin, or feminine

* Ascendant: *Children who are born during the two-hour segment of the day ruled by the Ox sign will have this sign as their ascendant and will display affinity for people born under this particular sign, as well as have many of the distinct character traits that identify the Ox sign.*

FIVE CYCLES* OF THE LUNAR YEARS OF THE OX IN THE WESTERN CALENDAR

START DATE		END DATE	ELEMENT OF THE YEAR
February 15, 1961	to	February 4, 1962	Metal
February 3, 1973	to	January 22, 1974	Water
February 20, 1985	to	February 8, 1986	Wood
February 7, 1997	to	January 27, 1998	Fire
January 26, 2009	to	February 13, 2010	Earth

* A cycle on the lunar horoscope equals twelve years. Five cycles completes sixty years.

Note: One who is born on the day before the start of the lunar year of the Ox, e.g., February 19, 1985, will belong to the animal sign before the Ox, which is the Rat, the first lunar sign. One who is born on the day after the end of the lunar year of the Ox, e.g., February 9, 1986, will belong to the animal sign following the Ox, which is the Tiger, the third lunar sign.

THE OX SIGN

ALL THINGS COME TO HIM WHO WAITS

The Ox Personality

The second earth branch of the Chinese lunar cycle is named *Chou* and symbolized by the Ox. The *Chou* branch is a sign of strength, and likewise a child born in its year will display the characteristic traits of dependability, integrity, and industriousness. Early in life the *Chou*, or Ox, personality, displays a sense of purpose in everything she does. She tends to be methodical and is a creature of habit. By the age of five, her ways will be quite set. She knows what she likes and what she does not, and it will be hard to get her to change her mind. Definitely not a crybaby or whiner, she will apply herself diligently to any task and work until she masters it. One thing that you will notice about the Ox child is that she is patient, careful, and honest. She may or may not be talkative, but she has an intrinsic sense of privacy and will never openly boast or make ridiculous claims about her ability. If anything, she usually plays down her own merits and feels embarrassed if praised openly or put in the limelight. Responsive and obedient to authority, she could be shy and soft-spoken, but in reality she is very observant and determined. The Ox is competitive, but not in an outwardly fashion. She sets her own standards early in life, and these are the only standards she will try to excel in. Her resoluteness in achieving what she sets out to do or having things her way could sometimes make it difficult for her parents to achieve the closeness that they desire.

However, if they are patient with the Ox child, she will respond with steadfast devotion and a deep caring for her loved ones that no spoken words are needed to convey. She is willing to make sacrifices for her parents without ever talking about it. Her capacity for endurance and perseverance is admirable. But don't ever underestimate her in any way. Her silence does not mean consent, and she can be stubborn and unreasonable when thwarted by what she perceives as unfair or uncalled for. Unlikely to be very adventurous or daring, she has a conservative attitude and prefers the tried and true. With such a conservative attitude in life, she is averse to taking unnecessary risks with her money, time, or efforts.

She is efficient and likes to be organized and on schedule. Nothing irks the Ox child more than too many changes and disruptions in travel plans or her normal everyday schedule. Delays and even small setbacks or complications bring out the negative in her. She hates surprises but likes routine and a well-planned day. Anything unexpected or new will arouse her suspicions and cause her to overact. She is not adventurous in trying out new food or ways of doing things.

It takes time for her to adjust, so give her some leeway and don't push her too hard to make changes in what she is comfortable with. If she is a bit slow to catch on or change her ways to suit others, don't worry too much. Once she realizes that she is holding up the team, her pride in her own reputation as being a responsible and reliable team player will force her to work harder to meet your expectations.

The opinionated Ox child needs to learn the value of compromise and develop a sense of humor. She tends to be inflexible and too serious. Perhaps she needs to learn to divide priorities early in life so that she could be serious on serious issues. She could also allow herself to take it easy and laugh away small problems or minor issues that are not on the high-priority list. This would be better than to look at all problems as life-or-death issues. Her biggest challenge is learning to meet others halfway or admitting defeat. This should never be seen as a lack of strength or integrity, although the Ox child may believe otherwise. One who is able to reason and compromise is regarded as the bigger person, who has the strength and confidence to succeed in a gracious, nonconfrontational way.

Having an Ox child is a blessing because she is conscientious, self-motivated, and able to keep promises made without ever changing her mind or renegotiating the terms. Your deliberate and devoted Ox child will always be there for you. She is filial by nature and will allow her family to lean on her strong shoulders. Her word is her bond, and she is honest and forthright in every way. She rarely changes her mind and never wants anyone to feel sorry for her. A pillar of strength and energy in times of crisis, you can rely on your Ox child to stand by you through thick and thin. Don't think that just because she is quiet and unassuming that she does not have deep and lasting feelings. The Ox rarely shows her hurt or disappointment. Instead of complaining, she keeps such feelings inside, where they tend to grow, and as a result she may develop a cold or defensive nature in order to protect herself from more pain or disappointment.

Nothing dismays the Ox child more than knowing she has failed to meet the grade or that she has disappointed her parents in any way. She wants to succeed by her own merit and will strive valiantly to perform above expectations. If she fails, she hardly needs any criticism from anyone. She is her own harshest critic, and she tends to push herself at a relentless, merciless pace. Not one to take failure lightly, the Ox is a model of industry and unfailing determination.

Birth Order and Sibling Rivalry

*FIRSTBORN OR ONLY CHILD

When the Ox child is the firstborn or only child, she will be a quiet introvert who prefers to keep to herself. Neat, punctual, and very organized, she will not appreciate changes to her routine, and even if you get her consent, she will not be a happy trouper until things are back to normal. She does not fight to be the leader, unless she has a very strong ascendant. With her willpower, she will fight to have things her way and is quite intolerant of what others want if they are in conflict with what she believes is right. She tends to communicate only with those she likes and sometimes she sends the wrong message because of her failure to explain herself properly. She often does not give her real reason for wanting something and assumes that others should be able to read her mind. She tends to be strict with her younger siblings and could be a bit of a disciplinarian if they oppose her. At times, she could even be tougher than the parents are in enforcing the rules—no ifs, ands, or buts about it. Consequently, younger siblings rebel and constantly challenge her authority, especially if the next child is a year younger and born in the year of the rebellious and captivating Tiger.

* When a child is born five years after another child, he or she is also considered a firstborn child.

MIDDLE OR LATER-BORN CHILD

The Ox child may be more comfortable in the middle- or later-born position because she does not seek the limelight and does not enjoy being the center of attention. Obedient, diligent, and happy to be by herself, the middle- or later-born Ox personality does not have to blaze any trails or set any limits as the firstborn must do. She may prefer to stay in the shadow of the firstborn and peacefully stay out of controversy, working along peacefully. Parents do not have discipline problems with the Ox as a child, who prides herself as one who knows the rules and will abide by them. The Ox as the second or middle child does not question the authority of the firstborn and may be supportive if the firstborn is able to understand and bond with her.

YOUNGEST OR LAST-BORN CHILD

As a high achiever and an independent and competent worker, the Ox in the youngest position may feel irritated at times at being babied or doted on. She matures early and does not like too much cuddling. Self-motivated and determined to do things by herself and in her own way and time, she does not appreciate too much help from her elders. She considers it a lack of confidence if everyone in the family looks over her shoulders and helps her up every time she falls. She wants to be left alone with her own problems, and too much interference and concern from those who care about her actually cause her to become secretive and resistant to any advice given. Let her work at her own pace, make her own mistakes, and do not offer to help her unless she asks for your assistance. She wants to be taken seriously and will guard her own privacy. In this position, she sincerely believes that the best is last.

Ascendants

In Chinese horoscopes, the two-hour segment ruling the time of birth is known as the ascendant sign. This can also be referred to as the child's "inner self."

The time of birth used to determine the ascendant is always the local time in the place of birth.

For a child born in the Year of the Ox:

THE RAT ASCENDANT—TIME OF BIRTH IS BETWEEN 11 P.M. AND 12:59 A.M.

The charming Rat ascendant ensures this child will have no difficulty making friends. She will have a knack for communication and making people feel comfortable. The sociable lightheartedness that comes from the Rat ascendant makes this Ox more easygoing and adaptable. While flexible and affectionate, she may still need lessons in sharing and tolerance. This Ox child is quick to make comparisons and can have high and often unreachable standards. The Ox in her tends to be stubborn, but the Rat ascendant teaches this child the value of compromise and strategy. Her Rat inner self is outgoing and could mellow the Ox's toughness and seriousness.

THE OX ASCENDANT—TIME OF BIRTH IS BETWEEN 1 A.M. AND 2:59 A.M.

This double Ox combination produces a no-nonsense, get-things-done personality who has no time for foolish pursuits or anything that wastes her time. You can depend on this child to finish assignments and keep commitments. She is always on time. The model of a great work ethic, this dutiful child may actually need convincing to go outside and run through the sprinklers. She will need to learn to see the lighter side of things and have fun with peers. Lessons in public relations and diplomacy will help this child be more flexible, cooperative, and make new friends. Stable, dependable, and consistent, she is a pillar of strength. But she needs to develop a less serious outlook at life and put her own needs first.

THE TIGER ASCENDANT—TIME OF BIRTH IS BETWEEN 3 A.M. AND 4:59 A.M.

With the Tiger as her inner self, this Ox child is drawn to the stage or sports. She will enjoy taking part in activities where talents can be demonstrated and recognized. The Tiger brings out an impulsive fire and flair that other Oxen may lack. This child is anything but a wallflower; she will seek out whatever she fancies and will mostly succeed in obtaining it. Not as shy or humble as other Ox children, this child will vie for constant and undivided attention. She knows she has a lot to offer. The Ox part is solid, serious, and disciplined, while the Tiger inner self can be playful, daring, and dramatic. There won't be a dull moment in the house.

THE RABBIT ASCENDANT—TIME OF BIRTH IS BETWEEN 5 A.M. AND 6:59 A.M.

The Rabbit ascendant balances the Ox's personality by loosening the ultra-overachiever mind-set. The Ox can often work without any breaks, but this child will be sure to set aside time for both work and play. This child will be the ideal friend—loyal, trustworthy, and a good listener. First impressions are crucial to this child, and she will not part with them easily. Although she does not openly disagree with others or stick to opinions, the child has a mind of her own and will not change her beliefs easily. The Rabbit's inner self is more able to control the Ox's temper and stubbornness. A diplomatic and cooperative child when she wants to be, the Rabbit ascendant will ensure that the Ox personality gets what she is after without too much confrontation with others.

THE DRAGON ASCENDANT—TIME OF BIRTH IS BETWEEN 7 A.M. AND 8:59 A.M.

This child will have a healthy self-esteem and confidence from day one, with the Dragon in charge of her inner self. She will have a take-charge attitude marked by the Dragon's passion and intensity. The Ox sign makes sure that the job will always get done, but often at some great costs with the ambitious Dragon influence. This Ox is not as calm and introverted as others are, because this ascendant is outgoing by nature and needs to be with friends and supporters. Sports and other group activities may develop cooperation and teamwork, which the Dragon inner self excels in. The Ox has great strength of character and capacity for hard work and dedication, and the shining Dragon ascendant reinforces these positive traits.

THE SNAKE ASCENDANT—TIME OF BIRTH IS BETWEEN 9 A.M. AND 10:59 A.M.

The Snake ascendant and secretive Ox make this child a bank vault when it comes to keeping a secret. She will be fiercely private and independent, choosing to spend the day inside alone with her thoughts if she does not like the company of certain people. Naturally spiritual and introspective, this child will not waver in her thoughts and convictions. Others will respect such faith and complexity, but some may not be able to unravel such a mystery. Her great faith in herself comes from never doubting her intuition and natural ability to figure things out for herself. The Snake ascendant brings great ambition into this Ox child's life, and she will go far.

THE HORSE ASCENDANT—TIME OF BIRTH IS BETWEEN 11 A.M. AND 12:59 P.M.

The carefree and adventurous Horse ascendant could make arts and travel capture the imagination of this child early in life. She will enjoy music and tales of far-off lands and brave conquests. Independent and bold, the Ox child with the Horse inside her is not likely to be shy or secretive. This child will be a joy to watch grow up, with laughter and dancing always surrounding her. However, the attention span of this child will be short, as she prefers variety and spice in life. She may need to learn to pay attention and focus on one thing at a time. This Ox child will still value discipline and have a strong, dependable character, but the inner self of the Horse ascendant brings humor, daring, and adventure into her personality.

THE SHEEP ASCENDANT—TIME OF BIRTH IS BETWEEN 1 P.M. AND 2:59 P.M.

The Sheep's inner self gives this combination stability and a generous heart. This child will be a softer and sweeter Ox than others can be. She will be creative and inventive, open to new ways of thought. She will have an innate ability to make things beautiful and work with others. The Ox-Sheep heart is a pure one indeed, producing a selfless listener who may grow up to spend countless hours on the phone to counsel and console others. This child may also spend money freely, but the Ox within can be awakened to curb lavish spending and impulsive decision making. This is a cooperative, more emotional Ox who has expensive tastes and loves refinement, art, and music.

THE MONKEY ASCENDANT—TIME OF BIRTH IS BETWEEN 3 P.M. AND 4:59 P.M.

This child's natural ambition will surface early, in the form of all sorts of enterprising endeavors—not surprising with the skills of the Monkey as her inner self. She will have her own lemonade stand in a high-traffic area or the prize for the school's top chocolate salesperson. A natural strategist, she is patient and observant. No opportunity will get by if she can find a way to benefit from it. Watch out, this child will be charming and able to get out of sticky situations, but then again the Ox personality obeys and respects the law and does not opt for shortcuts, which her Monkey other self tends to favor. The Monkey ascendant teaches the steady Ox that there is more than one way to do things, and often more than one correct answer to any problem. A more creative and resourceful Ox personality, indeed.

THE ROOSTER ASCENDANT—TIME OF BIRTH IS BETWEEN 5 P.M. AND 6:59 P.M.

The Rooster as the inner self makes this child form fixed and firm opinions on everything under the sun early in life. Peers of this child will be quick to notice that this is not someone who will back down from anything. Unlike other oxen, the Rooster ascendant could make this Ox more critical and exacting than she already is. She will be a flawless debater and may find herself running for student office or other positions of responsibility. The flamboyant Rooster brings more color and excitement into the Ox's natural love for order and principles, and she is able to lead with great self-confidence and aplomb.

THE DOG ASCENDANT—TIME OF BIRTH IS BETWEEN 7 P.M. AND 8:59 P.M.

The friendly Dog and the strong Ox combination create the ultimate team player. She will be an objective thinker, choosing to rely upon instincts and not following the crowd, but fair and reliable. While this child will be disciplined and independent, she has a real soft spot for those in need. She will have a natural desire to help others and befriend causes others have given up or forgotten about. The Dog ascendant knows how to listen and provides this Ox child with a natural warm personality that is supportive and friendly without being overbearing or judgmental.

THE BOAR ASCENDANT—TIME OF BIRTH IS BETWEEN 9 P.M. AND 10:59 P.M.
This Ox child will know both how to save and how to spend with the Boar's influence guiding her inner self. She will know her taste and personal style early and waste no time in communicating it to others and the rest of the world. Though fun-loving and generous, this child will be no pushover and could be very stubborn when she is challenged. She will take on responsibility early in life; giving her word is really a serious thing that will be honored. The Ox's innate, uncompromising, and determined mind-set is softened by the Boar ascendant's traits of kindness and generosity. Still, others should be careful not to push this child too far and take advantage of her, because they will be surprised when the Ox-Boar personality loses her patience.

Famous Persons Born in the Year of the Ox

Walt Disney
King Leopold III
Sammy Davis Jr.
Richard Burton
Melina Mercouri
Dustin Hoffman
King Juan Carlos of Spain
Colin Powell
Gerald Ford
Vincent Van Gogh
Charlie Chaplin
Hans Christian Andersen
Jack Lemmon
Bruce Springsteen
Meryl Streep

Emperor Hirohito
Gore Vidal
Peter Sellers
Dame Margaret Thatcher
Robert Redford
Boris Spassky
Bill Cosby
Richard Nixon
Archbishop Makarios of Greece
Carlo Ponti
Jawaharlal Nehru
Johann Sebastian Bach
Napoleon Bonaparte
Anthony Hopkins
Princess Diana

As a treat to your child, please read the Ox's story,
"How the Ox Got His Horns," which follows.

THE OX'S STORY

"HOW THE OX GOT HIS HORNS"

In a little village high up in the mountains, there lived a ten-year-old boy and his widowed mother. They had a plot of land along the steps of the mountain, left by the boy's father, who had gone off to war and died in valiant battle. The other farming families all had oxen and horses to help with the plowing of their fields, but the young boy and his mother lived a hard and bitter life without the aid of any farm animal to help them work the land.

Oxen in those days resembled horses, only they were bigger and stronger and had better tempers. The boy loved Oxen and would always look at the Oxen of his neighbors and say to his mother, "How I wish I could have my own Ox, Mother."

"Foolish lad," said his mother. "Do not wish for things you cannot hope to have. Can't you see that we are poor? Where will we ever get enough money to buy an Ox?"

"I understand, Mother," sighed the boy, "but, still I can dream and wish, can't I?"

In the poor village high in the mountains, children did not go to school. They were not taught to read or write, instead they were expected to learn about the land so that they could become farmers like their parents and their parents before them. So, the boy began drawing charcoal pictures of Oxen in the dirt, on slabs of stone, and even on pieces of bamboo for paper was expensive and unavailable. He became so good at drawing Oxen that he began to draw them bigger and bigger. Finally, he was able to draw a life-size Ox on one wall of their hut. The boy worked diligently, drawing every hair of the Ox, and as he drew in the ears and eyes and mouth, he talked and sang to his charcoal picture, telling it how much fun they could have together and how kindly he would treat his Ox.

"You'll be my best friend and the brother I never had and the father I lost," the boy whispered to his Ox drawing. "We'll do everything together."

As he fell asleep on the night after he completed his Ox picture, the gods in heaven took pity on the young lad and decided to bring his drawing of an Ox to life. His wish was so sincere and pure. When the boy awoke the next morning, he was surprised and overjoyed to find a big and gentle Ox licking his cheek. The boy and his mother could not believe their good fortune. The Ox helped them work on the small plot of land to raise grain and it carried away rocks and boulders to make room for a larger area to plant other crops and even some fruit trees. In the evenings, the boy would take the Ox inside the hut, as it was their most precious possession. The boy enjoyed singing and talking to his Ox, who always listened quietly and patiently.

Word about the beautiful Ox traveled to the next village. After a year or so, a group of men came to see the young lad and his mother. They offered to buy the Ox for their master, the Duke of Yore. Of course, the boy and his mother refused and said that no amount of gold would make them part with their beloved Ox. Thereupon, the men became angry and took out strong ropes, which they tied around the neck of the gentle Ox, and dragged it away with the help of their horses.

The boy cried and pleaded, but the men beat and kicked him when he tried to stand in their way. His poor mother was powerless to help or protect him, as the evil men from Yore pushed her to the ground. Without the help of their faithful Ox, the boy and his mother were soon destitute and returned to working on the land by themselves again. As winter came, the boy's mother became ill and could no longer help him work.

The boy thought more and more of his beloved Ox and missed it greatly. One evening as the snow fell, the boy started drawing again and soon he drew another life-size Ox on the same wall of his hut. All week long he did his best to remember every detail of his Ox, but when he finally had to dot the eyes to bring the Ox to life, the boy could not complete the task. He felt he was being disloyal to his first Ox, who had been both his brother and best friend. As the

33

THE OX'S STORY

boy wept for his lost Ox, he fell asleep and had a strange dream. The boy dreamt that his Ox came to him and spoke.

"Please do not cry, little brother. I will soon return to you. But first you must do something to help me break free from these bad people who have kept me a prisoner. When you wake up, you must draw a pair of strong horns on my head in your picture. Have faith, I will find a way to come home."

The young boy awoke and immediately set out to do exactly what his Ox told him in the dream. After he finished drawing the horns, the boy dotted the eyes of the Ox and could swear that the eyes twinkled as though the Ox recognized him. The boy's mother did not approve of the boy's drawing of the second Ox and told him so.

"Do not tempt fate again, my son," she pleaded. "Another Ox would bring about misfortune and heartbreak for us again. We are destined to remain poor and work hard all our lives. There is no other fate for us, my son."

The boy did not argue with his mother but sat in quiet determination all day as he prayed with all his heart for the Ox to come home. As night fell, mother and son crawled under their thick winter quilts and soon both fell asleep. In the morning, when the boy and his mother awoke, the picture of the Ox had disappeared from the wall as before. Outside the hut, they heard a low mooing that was the familiar voice of their beloved friend. They opened their door and there outside the hut stood their beloved Ox with some ropes still around its neck but also blood on its horns.

From that time on, the gods saw the wisdom of the Ox's need for horns and gave all the other Oxen and buffaloes horns to protect themselves against those who would mistreat them. Reunited, the boy and his mother lived happily with their Ox for a very long time. The Ox once again brought them prosperity and security, and they never ever saw the evil men of Yore again.

虎

CHAPTER THREE
THE TIGER

The Third Lunar Sign

The Tiger is a delightful paradox,

All the world is his stage.

He is the colorful trailblazer,

Always seeking the unattainable,

Trying the untried.

He dances to life's music

In joyous abandon.

Hailed the unparalleled performer.

The Tiger is courage, power, and

Daring.

His motto is: **CURIOSITY FINDS KNOWLEDGE**

THE TIGER'S BRANCH

CHINESE NAME FOR THE TIGER: *Hu*

RANK: Third

HOURS OF THE TIGER: From 3 A.M. to 4:59 A.M.*

DIRECTION OF THIS BRANCH: East-northeast

SEASON AND PRINCIPAL MONTH: Winter and February

CORRESPONDS TO THE WESTERN SIGN: Aquarius, the Water Bearer

FIXED ELEMENT: Wood

STEM: Yang, or masculine

* Ascendant: *Children who are born during the two-hour segment of the day ruled by the Tiger sign will have this sign as their ascendant and will display affinity for people born under this particular sign, as well as have many of the distinct character traits that identify the Tiger sign.*

FIVE CYCLES* OF THE LUNAR YEARS OF THE TIGER IN THE WESTERN CALENDAR

START DATE		END DATE	ELEMENT OF THE YEAR
February 5, 1962	to	January 24, 1963	Water
January 23, 1974	to	February 10, 1975	Wood
February 9, 1986	to	January 28, 1987	Fire
January 28, 1998	to	February 15, 1999	Earth
February 14, 2010	to	February 2, 2011	Metal

* A cycle on the lunar horoscope equals twelve years. Five cycles completes sixty years.

Note: One who is born on the day before the start of the lunar year of the Tiger, e.g., January 27, 1998, will belong to the animal sign before the Tiger, which is the Ox, the second lunar sign. One who is born on the day after the end of the lunar year of the Tiger, e.g., February 16, 1999, will belong to the animal sign following the Tiger, which is the Rabbit, the fourth lunar sign.

THE TIGER SIGN

CURIOSITY FINDS KNOWLEDGE

The Tiger Personality

The third earth branch of the Chinese lunar cycle is formally named *Yin* and its sign is the Tiger. A child born under the *Yin* branch is an incurable idealist. He interacts with everyone with vitality and genuine interest. Never halfhearted about anything, he always has an opinion and makes an impression. One never comes away from a vivacious Tiger child without being affected in some way. The bright and enthusiastic child of the third earth branch could be a bundle of joy and a whirlwind at the same time. He sparkles with activity, although it is hard to hold his interest for long periods of time. However, if he has a good and patient parent or teacher, the Tiger child could be molded into the model of deportment. This is because he enjoys role-playing and understands how important it is to play his part well. As a trouper and real performer, he is par excellence. Tiger children tend to be hyperactive and inquisitive. Not one to keep anything inside, he is expressive about the way he feels and thinks. It will be difficult to suppress his natural curiosity and gregarious character.

The positive side of his personality is that he is able to vent his anger and feelings quite easily and could go on after a tantrum as if nothing happened. He does not bottle up his emotions, so you will know exactly when and why he is acting up. His assertive and aggressive personality tends to dominate the household and other siblings and even parents have to play second fiddle when the Tiger is on the prowl. The Tiger child could also be impulsive and demanding and tends to change his mind without much notice. However, he is always open to new ideas and will not hesitate to try something first before making up his mind.

The vibrant Tiger child needs good role models coupled with discipline and love. His warm and idealistic heart needs to see the good in others because he is by nature a humanitarian. He has to give of himself and contribute whatever he can for the good of others, and he will always be drawn to a cause (just or unjust) where he can channel his irrepressible energies. When he is able to focus and direct his many talents where they will be most beneficial, the Tiger is incomparable. When he is left to his own devices and drifts from one project to another, he can be difficult to control or understand. Good at public relations and communications, the Tiger is never at a loss for words. Spontaneous in his actions and thoughts, the Tiger is easy to love and appreciate. He must learn at an early age how to approach problems in a rational and calm manner and refrain from hysterics and dramatic outbursts. Let him work himself out and his ranting and raving and scenes will be storms in a teacup, where he could exaggerate things to a higher degree to make himself more important and his pain more intense.

It is hard to ever ignore the Tiger child because he is a very giving soul and has the best of intentions. Supportive and sympathetic, he is easily touched by the pain of others and can be very unselfish when called upon to help. However, one must guide the Tiger child to get over his love of procrastination and vacillating tendencies. He likes to wait to the last minute before making his final commitment, and even then he could still change his mind. This may just about drive his parents and teachers crazy, but the fact remains that the Tiger examines all the options in front of him, and let's face it—he wants it *all*. If the Tiger learns to make quick decisions and stick by them and to focus his valuable energy and time to the task at hand, he will be a roaring success.

A natural entertainer, he will never lack admirers and an audience. He loves to put up a show and sometimes is not too objective when it comes to being realistic. Because of his oversized ego and sense of importance, the Tiger finds it hard to compromise or cooperate with others and tends to hog the limelight. He is the same with the affection of his parents. He wants the biggest share and will try to dominate his parents' attention if he can.

Birth Order and Sibling Rivalry

*FIRSTBORN OR ONLY CHILD

The Tiger in this position tends to emphasize his own importance. He will strive to be the best at everything to show younger siblings or his parents how smart and really intelligent he is. It will be hard to surpass his showmanship

* When a child is born five years after another child, he or she is also considered a firstborn child.

and ability to hold everyone's attention. This could be very intimidating to younger siblings. He could be kind, thoughtful, and loving to his siblings, provided they know their place and play supporting roles with the Tiger as the star. At school, he will excel and vie for the approval of his teachers. The Tiger is self-motivated and is really a little soldier at heart. He has to keep fighting battles to prove his own worthiness and importance. He works hard because he can't let others outshine him in anything.

MIDDLE OR LATER-BORN CHILD

The Tiger as the second or middle child will be the adventurer and the rebel of the family. He will be the risk taker and precocious fighter. Independent and unconventional, he could be unpredictable but brilliant in his way of dealing with people and in communications. In this position, the Tiger child will try to take over the firstborn's place from day one. Whether consciously or unconsciously, he will want to be number one and will always be nipping at the ankles of his older sibling, trying to displace or outshine him. This could develop into a friendly rivalry or a more serious competition, depending on his ascendant. To younger siblings, the Tiger as the middle child is generous and helpful because he does not view them as a threat and loves to play the role of their protector and savior.

YOUNGEST OR LAST-BORN CHILD

As the youngest and the last born, the Tiger child is everyone's darling. He can do no wrong, and he knows it. A little enchanter, he will have the older ones eating out of his hand. He knows early in life the power he holds over the older siblings and over his parents. They will adore and dote on this colorful personality who won't disappoint when it comes to holding their undivided attention and the strings to their hearts. When the Tiger is pampered and paid attention to, he does the opposite and could become very thoughtful and giving. He is able to forge warm and strong relationships early in life and can be counted on to be courageous, optimistic, and devoted to his family.

Ascendants

In Chinese horoscopes, the two-hour segment ruling the time of birth is known as the ascendant sign. This can also be referred to as the child's "inner self."

The time of birth used to determine the ascendant is always the local time in the place of birth.

For a child born in the Year of the Tiger:

THE RAT ASCENDANT—TIME OF BIRTH IS BETWEEN 11 P.M. AND 12:59 A.M.
This child with the Rat ascendant will have a taste for excitement and a love of drama. He may quarrel with family and friends one day and on the next wonder what everyone is still upset about. Although he is not insensitive, it will be difficult for this child to get a handle on his emotions. He wants to eat his cake and keep it, too. This child loves to be challenged and will enjoy debating and questioning everything and everyone he is interested in. As a vibrant Tiger, he will be impulsive and daring, but the Rat ascendant may very well encourage some healthy caution, deep thought, and need for security.

THE OX ASCENDANT—TIME OF BIRTH IS BETWEEN 1 A.M. AND 2:59 A.M.
A Tiger with the Ox ascendant is more calm and collected than most. Not likely to fly off the handle as quickly as other Tigers, he will be more dependable and consistent in work habits. Though this child can be seen as quiet and dutiful, he does know his limits and will not let others take undue advantage. Funny how all of a sudden, one so obedient and cooperative can put others in their place in a soft-spoken but firm way. The Ox temper balances out the lively Tiger, poising this child for responsibility at an earlier age than most.

THE TIGER ASCENDANT—TIME OF BIRTH IS BETWEEN 3 A.M. AND 4:59 A.M.
With a double dose of Tiger energy, this child with a Tiger ascendant cannot help but be a natural firecracker. With the enhanced positive characteristics of

the Tiger—confidence, strength, and unbeatable charm—combined with the negative personality traits of a fierce temper and occasional carelessness, this child will keep everyone in suspense. He may embark on many adventures, but always be assured that whether hit or miss, this child will go on undaunted. This child will never be in need of a pep talk. His ego is larger than life and there will be a great deal of excitement wherever he goes and whatever he does.

THE RABBIT ASCENDANT—TIME OF BIRTH IS BETWEEN 5 A.M. AND 6:59 A.M.
The Rabbit ascendant invokes serenity and practicality into the feisty Tiger. This child will still love adventure and excitement, but the Rabbit's innocence and fun-loving personality encourages finding life's more simple blessings. A responsible decision maker and natural mediator, he likes to avoid controversy. Though soft-spoken and polite, this child will always be on the lookout for a chance to benefit from any situation. The Rabbit ascendant gives this child more polish and composure. He will be able to hold his temper, yet he could still pounce on you when you least expect him.

THE DRAGON ASCENDANT—TIME OF BIRTH IS BETWEEN 7A.M. AND 8:59 A.M.
The Dragon and the Tiger make for a passionate heart that is more ruled by emotions than reason. This child is not easily reasoned with when he has his heart set on something. Whether in sports or a social cause, this child will fight for what he believes in no matter what the odds. Naturally competitive, this Tiger-Dragon child may get upset when things do not go his way. A great PR and salesperson, he will campaign tirelessly for what he wants, so be prepared for a long struggle if you have to go against such a dynamic personality. Group activities and team sports could teach this child that one cannot win all the time, but you know he will never stop trying. With such a strong spirit, this child will naturally gain recognition and respect and be a trendsetter with great influence.

THE SNAKE ASCENDANT—TIME OF BIRTH IS BETWEEN 9 A.M. AND 10:59 A.M.
The Snake within makes this Tiger a discreet and observant child. The Snake ascendant encourages the Tiger to think for the long term, rather than the short

term, which is an invaluable trait. This child is careful and gifted in judging both character and environments and will be especially cautious and open-minded in his exploration. However, both the Snake ascendant and the Tiger are suspicious by nature, and this child could be a bit of a detective who will never just take people's word for anything without verifying and doing some research on his own. A good student and supportive friend, the Tiger child is able to keep confidences and learns to weigh his position carefully before jumping to conclusions. He does not like to give advice, but may also be averse to taking advice when he most needs it.

THE HORSE ASCENDANT—TIME OF BIRTH IS BETWEEN 11 A.M. AND 12:59 P.M.
The Horse and the Tiger are two signs that know how to enjoy life, and with such charm, how could they not? The happy Horse ascendant and the vivacious Tiger dance to the same beat. Naturally independent and confident, this child's obsession will be new experiences, sports, and involvement with electronics, computers, and any new technology that fires his amazing imagination. A lover of speed and action, he will be a great traveler with the Horse's self-preserving personality, but may be careless in other arenas of life. It may be comforting to know that throughout all of these adventures, he will never be alone, because wherever he goes, friends will always be found. This child is able to adapt to any situation without much complaint and form practical relationships that will serve him well.

THE SHEEP ASCENDANT—TIME OF BIRTH IS BETWEEN 1 P.M. AND 2:59 P.M.
Strangers may underestimate this well-behaved child, but a parent and close friends will know that he is a quiet storm waiting to erupt. Born to create and with an innate knowledge of what is prized and valuable, others will admire this child's talents. He will be ambitious and work hard to craft his skills, but with a Sheep ascendant, this Tiger child is not as domineering or aggressive as others. Many will probably comment to you on what a pleasure your child is to teach and be around. Beneath this grace and diplomacy lie great strength and a kind heart that values friendships and family above material possessions.

THE MONKEY ASCENDANT—TIME OF BIRTH IS BETWEEN 3 P.M. AND 4:59 P.M.

The Tiger's fire and the Monkey's crafty intelligence make sure all signs point to "yes." This little dynamo will not take "no" for an answer. He has a good solution for every one of his problems. Who knows how high a child with this much intelligence and passion can go? Ready for any opportunity, he will take on any task with great confidence and a positive attitude. He will deal with setbacks well, learning from past mistakes and thinking of new strategies for success. The Tiger and the Monkey are often at two different extremes, but it can be quite a blessing to have such well-matched opponents tame one another.

THE ROOSTER ASCENDANT—TIME OF BIRTH IS BETWEEN 5 P.M. AND 6:59 P.M.

The Rooster inner self has a love affair with order and craves perfection. The volatile Tiger takes cues from emotion and could be impulsive when not guided by his parents or teachers. This commanding child will pack a powerful punch, always standing at center stage. He will be ambitious and is drawn to the limelight, but as a Tiger his approval ratings move up and down with the weather. Undeterred by failures and setbacks, this child is drawn to power and leadership. The Tiger and Rooster merge dedication, passion, and order to getting things done. A commanding yet complicated personality who may be very opinionated.

THE DOG ASCENDANT—TIME OF BIRTH IS BETWEEN 7 P.M. AND 8:59 P.M.

This personable child is a natural in social situations, blessed with many friends and a charming, likeable attitude. The Dog teaches the Tiger that fair play and consideration can go a longer way than throwing a fit. A child with this combination will not ignore any injustice and will rush to help anyone in need. He will defend friends and classmates against bullies and will stand up for his rights. Articulate and a gifted communicator, the Tiger child has wit and humor and a keen knowledge on how to bring out the best in others. The loyal Dog ascendant brings sensibility and stability to this child, while the Tiger fosters an imagination that can never be rivaled.

THE BOAR ASCENDANT—TIME OF BIRTH IS BETWEEN 9 P.M. AND 10:59 P.M.

The Boar as the inner self brings out a powerful Tiger child who is generous and loving. With this combination, the passionate Tiger child will live to make friends and family happy and comfortable. He will have the sensuous Boar's appetite for the good life, never passing up any opportunity to smell the roses and taste the wine. He must watch the appetite in all aspects of his life: food, romance, career, and marriage. The Tiger and the Boar combination create a child with great ambition who is always willing to go the distance. When he is happy, he tends to be overly optimistic, and when he is disappointed, he acts as if it were the end of the world. Parents and teachers must teach this Tiger to find the middle of the road and to deal with setbacks in a more mature and accepting way. He must believe that there will always be another chance or another conquest in which he could succeed or redeem failures of the past.

Famous Persons Born in the Year of the Tiger

Charles de Gaulle	Ho Chi-Minh
Ludwig van Beethoven	Dwight D. Eisenhower
Princess Anne	Simon Bolivar
Queen Elizabeth II	Emily Dickinson
St. Francis Xavier	Marilyn Monroe
Tom Cruise	Kenny Rogers
Liv Ullman	Oscar Wilde
Stevie Wonder	Francisco de Goya
Niccolo Paganini	Marco Polo
Richard Branson	Agatha Christie

As a treat to your child, please read the Tiger's story,
"How the Tiger Got His Stripes," which follows.

THE TIGER'S STORY

"HOW THE TIGER GOT HIS STRIPES"

Many, many thousands of years ago when the world was very young, when animals could talk and humans could understand them, there lived a very curious Tiger. This Tiger was a handsome creature, all gold and orange with a thick, long, elegant tail that dragged proudly behind him.

One day, while he was loitering around, the Tiger came upon a farm and saw an Ox pulling a plow and working very hard. A man stood above the plow, driving the Ox. The poor Ox was straining all his muscles and dripping with sweat in the midday sun. His tongue was hanging out in thirst, yet he patiently worked for the man who was driving the poor Ox without any mercy.

After a while, the man hitched the Ox to a tree and went off toward his village to have his meal. The Tiger approached the exhausted Ox and asked him, "How could you let the man treat you this way?"

"You, Mr. Ox, are much bigger and stronger than that puny human," continued the Tiger. "You could easily gore him with your horns or kick and trample him with your powerful hoofs. Yet you let him put a yoke around your shoulders and toil so hard for him in the hot sun."

The big Ox shook his head sadly and replied.

"Yes, you may laugh and sneer at me, Mr. Tiger, but obviously you don't know too much about humans. The man may be small and weak compared to me, but he has a very valuable weapon that he could use against me if I do not obey his commands."

"A valuable weapon?" asked the curious Tiger. "What is that?"

"The man calls it 'his wits,' " answered the Ox.

"The man always says, 'I'll use my wits to get around this problem,' or he'll say to himself, 'No one is any match for my wits.' Or, 'I can use my wits to conquer anything or anyone.' So you see, Mr. Tiger, I'm afraid of the human and certainly don't want him to get angry and use his wits against me," said the Ox.

"What do these wits look like? Have you even seen the human's wits, which you are so afraid of, Mr. Ox?" questioned the Tiger.

"I dunno," said the Ox, "but sometimes he says he must sharpen his wits and other times he laughs at his friend who he says has dull wits."

"Hmm," thought the Tiger to himself, as he left the Ox and went on his way, "I must get some of those wits for myself. Even the strong and powerful Ox is afraid of that tiny human because of that valuable weapon, called wits. Well, I must be sure to make the man give me some."

So the next day, the Tiger waited for the same man to pass through a wooded area of the forest on his way to cut firewood, and the Tiger jumped out right in front of the man and demanded, "Hey, I heard about your wits and I would like to have some!"

"Why, Mr. Tiger, you startled me so!" said the man. "A lovely, good morning to you. Of course you can have some of my wits. But, unfortunately, I did not carry any with me today. I left them at home, since I did not think I would be using wits today."

"Why don't you go back home and fetch them?" asked the Tiger. "I really would like to have some, and I won't leave until you give me those wits."

"Fine," answered the man, "I'm quite willing to go back home and get the wits, but what if you are just playing a trick on me and you won't even be here when I return?"

"Of course I shall be here," said the Tiger. "I promise I won't leave."

"No, that won't do," insisted the man. "You must permit me to tie you to that big, old tree, so I can be absolutely sure you will be here when I get back. I shall not go to all the trouble of going home and bringing you my valuable wits if you don't agree."

The Tiger wanted the wits so badly that he agreed to let the man tie him to the tree with a long, stout rope.

"I won't be long," said the man as he hurried off.

Shortly after, the man returned with a torch and he started piling firewood around the Tiger. Then he lit a fire right under the Tiger.

"What are you doing?" shouted the Tiger as he struggled to free himself from the ropes.

"Using my wits, you foolish Tiger," shouted the man back.

"But, but, you said you would give me some wits," said the frightened Tiger. "Where are those wits you promised?"

"In my head, silly beast. My wits are invisible and I keep them inside my head. I wouldn't and couldn't give you any wits if I wanted to, but, of course, I don't," laughed the man as he walked away.

As the fire started burning the dry wood and the ropes, long black stripes covered the Tiger's lovely golden coat and he thought that he would surely be burned to death. The Tiger realized that Mr. Ox was right, after all, in being afraid of the man and his formidable wits. The Tiger regretted not believing the Ox and having crossed paths with the man.

But, then, out of nowhere came a young boy to his rescue. The boy swiftly cut the burning ropes and set the Tiger free before the flames started to burn his entire coat. The boy also carried a small bucket of water and washed the Tiger's face with the water.

"Thank you, thank you!" gasped the Tiger, as the boy let him drink from the bucket. "I was afraid I was done for. I suppose I was stupid to demand that the man give me his wits."

"Don't be afraid, Mr. Tiger," said the young boy quietly. "There is another thing we humans have that is almost as good as wits, and it is called kindness. What I just did for you was an act of kindness. We don't keep kindness in our heads, where we keep our wits. We keep kindness in our hearts, where it is more needed."

The Tiger and the boy parted ways, after they had put out the fire. From that time, the Tiger decided it was safer to go live up in the hills, where he had a better vantage point to watch the movements of the humans in the flatlands below. He did not want to cross paths with men again.

Years went by and the young boy grew up to be a clever and successful merchant. He often traveled over the hills and mountains where the Tiger

roamed. He would carry beautiful silks and porcelain and all kinds of goods in his special wagon pulled by two horses. He traveled to distant towns and villages to buy and sell things.

One day, a group of bandits waited to ambush the young merchant and rob him. They sprung out of their hiding places and made a surprise attack on the young man in broad daylight. The young man tried bravely to defend himself, but he was alone and seven bandits surrounded him from all sides.

The merchant thought his prosperous journeys had certainly come to an end, but then they all heard a fearsome roar as a big, striped Tiger jumped on top of the bandits and chased them away. Or, rather, the bandits fled for their lives.

"You are the boy who saved me from the fire," said the Tiger. "I've come to repay your kindness."

"Thank you, thank you, Mr. Tiger! I owe you my life!" bowed the grateful young man.

"I may not have those wits," winked the Tiger, "but I haven't forgotten about the gift of kindness." And with that, the Tiger disappeared back into the forest.

When the young man returned to his village, he had an artist draw a life-size portrait of the Tiger, complete with all the black stripes. The young man told everyone he met that the Tiger saved his life and that a Tiger was a symbol of courage and daring and could frighten away bandits and evil with his fearsome roar. And from that time on, the Tiger was regarded as an animal of strength and kindness. Many copied the merchant's example both then and now, by keeping a picture of the beautiful Tiger to protect their homes and along journeys.

CHAPTER FOUR

THE RABBIT

The Fourth Lunar Sign

The Rabbit is in tune with the

World around her yet she has her own

Private universe.

Quiet and peace loving

She heeds the inner voice of her soul.

A pleasant and tactful negotiator

The Rabbit is a strategist who subdues

By her ability to conform.

A good listener, the Rabbit

Sees both sides with clarity and

Is impartial and refined in her approach.

The Rabbit person appreciates

Harmony and inner peace.

She is the master of her own mind

And holds a sensitive heart within.

Her motto is: **DISCRETION IS THE KEY TO HAPPINESS AND HARMONY!**

THE RABBIT'S BRANCH

CHINESE NAME FOR THE RABBIT: *Tù*

RANK: Fourth

HOURS OF THE RABBIT: From 5 A.M. to 6:59 A.M.*

DIRECTION OF THIS BRANCH: Directly east

SEASON AND PRINCIPAL MONTH: Spring and March

CORRESPONDS TO THE WESTERN SIGN: Pisces, the Fish

FIXED ELEMENT: Wood

STEM: Yin, or feminine

* Ascendant: *Children who are born during the two-hour segment of the day ruled by the Rabbit sign will have this sign as their ascendant and will display affinity for people born under this particular sign as, well as have many of the distinct character traits that identify the Rabbit sign.*

FIVE CYCLES* OF THE LUNAR YEARS OF THE RABBIT IN THE WESTERN CALENDAR

START DATE		END DATE	ELEMENT OF THE YEAR
January 25, 1963	to	February 12, 1964	Water
February 11, 1975	to	January 30, 1976	Wood
January 29, 1987	to	February 16, 1988	Fire
February 16, 1999	to	February 4, 2000	Earth
February 3, 2011	to	January 22, 2012	Metal

* A cycle on the lunar horoscope equals twelve years. Five cycles completes sixty years.

Note: One who is born on the day before the start of the lunar year of the Rabbit, e.g., February 15, 1999, will belong to the animal sign before the Rabbit, which is the Tiger, the third lunar sign. One who is born on the day after the end of the lunar year of the Rabbit, e.g., February 5, 2000, will belong to the animal sign following the Rabbit, which is the Dragon, the fifth lunar sign.

THE RABBIT SIGN

DISCRETION IS THE KEY TO HAPPINESS AND HARMONY

The Rabbit Personality

The fourth earth branch of the Chinese lunar cycle is named *Mao* and is symbolized by the Rabbit. This is the sign of the peace-loving negotiator who values tranquility and equilibrium. The *Mao* personality hates conflict and discord and tends to distance herself from unpleasant situations and confrontation with others. She is usually a model baby and child and although she is alert and intelligent, she manages to keep out of trouble by being observant. The child born in the year of the fourth earth branch is a sensitive soul prone to being easily upset by loud noises, too much stimulation, and inordinate attention. She wants her own time and space. This child could be responsive and very quick in taking cues and will not miss a beat. Outwardly, she may appear shy and reticent, but in reality this personality is self-assured and gifted in many ways. She likes to maintain a modest, even humble stance and knows how to get along with her peers as well as her parents and teachers. It takes a while for the Rabbit child to open up or speak up about her wishes and opinions, but when she does, be aware that she has given everything careful thought and has considered her options in a detached and objective manner.

Because she presents such a composed and pleasant demeanor, people wrongly assume that the Rabbit child is a pushover. She is not. Although the Rabbit personality is not a confrontational one, she could be tough and swift in standing up for her rights. That outer appearance of conformity and grace covers up a superb sense of intuition and prudence. She can be patient and shrewd when it comes to getting things her way. She recognizes opportunity and will be ready to take advantage of it when the time is right. Calm and even serene under pressure, this amiable child is a go-getter who knows how not to step on other people's toes or get into trouble. Capable and self-assured in her own quiet way, she can be practical and resourceful. She tends to mature early and takes her responsibilities seriously.

When pushed to her limits, the Rabbit child becomes detached and aloof. She loses interest in pleasing her parents and shuts off all lines of communication until she can find a way out. She won't argue or complain too much, but could sulk and be very stubborn in her own unobtrusive way. She knows how to make her parents feel guilty without saying anything. Just a hurt look and stony silence will suffice. This way, she will wear her parents down skillfully and get her way without anyone losing too much face.

The reserved Rabbit child is a realist, although she may present an emotional and sensitive front. She is quick to assess what works for her and what doesn't, who loves her and who does not, whom to ask for help and whom to avoid, how to bend the rules carefully but not break any. At school, the Rabbit child is able to fend for herself and should not have trouble fitting in. An excellent student, she learns fast and with ease. She could act as a catalyst and influence changes and cooperation from others without having to change herself. The remarkable Rabbit child has unshakable faith in her own abilities and intelligence. Her parents may always be proud, as she will land on her feet with grace and confidence.

Birth Order and Sibling Rivalry

*FIRSTBORN OR ONLY CHILD

The Rabbit in this position does not take undue advantage of her position or superiority. She will strive to be helpful to younger siblings and show her parents how trustworthy and reliable she is. The Rabbit as the firstborn or only child is self-assured and will demand respect from her siblings as well as from her parents. She is supportive if they are able to follow her well-laid plans and value her excellent advice; otherwise, she could be difficult, manipulative, and condescending. The Rabbit child knows her strengths and weaknesses early in life and does not underestimate herself or overestimate others. Her siblings will know they can depend on her, and she has a soft spot for helping those less fortunate than her. She tends to worry and fret over little things and could get carried away in preparing for all unseen problems or contingencies. This position

* When a child is born five years after another child, he or she is also considered a firstborn child.

of responsibility heightens the Rabbit's need for security and harmony. She could become very controlling and bossy without meaning to.

MIDDLE OR LATER-BORN CHILD

The Rabbit as the middle child or a later born is really comfortable not being the center of attention as firstborn or only children are. In school, she will excel and earn the approval of her teachers and classmates. Self-motivated and obliging, she is not outwardly competitive and is able to work with everyone. She knows she accomplishes more by being nonconfrontational than by being rebellious. Even the firstborn will value the advice of the Rabbit who is a middle child. Supportive and wise, this Rabbit child is tolerant and understanding of others and is able to keep confidences. She will also keep her reservations to herself if her opinion is not sought. She loves to set a good example on how to do things properly and tends to be obedient and close to her parents. Level-headed and self-assured, this child is a good diplomat.

YOUNGEST OR LAST-BORN CHILD

As the youngest and the last born, the Rabbit child is a darling who needs to be protected, pampered, and cuddled. Be careful not to smother this Rabbit child. She is not as fragile as she looks. A little negotiator and mediator, she will have the older ones eating out of her hand. She knows early in life how to manage the older siblings and her parents. Honey is better bait than vinegar, and the little bunny is an expert at dishing out the honey. This personality works best if she is allowed to make her own choices early in life and given enough freedom to express herself. The Rabbit child in this unique position forms strong bonds early in life and can be counted on to be sensible, sensitive, and devoted to her loved ones.

Ascendants

In Chinese horoscopes, the two-hour segment ruling the time of birth is known as the ascendant sign. This can also be referred to as the child's "inner self."

The time of birth used to determine the ascendant is always the local time in the place of birth.

For a child born in the Year of the Rabbit:

THE RAT ASCENDANT—TIME OF BIRTH IS BETWEEN 11 P.M. AND 12:59 A.M.
A sweet blend of thoughtfulness and a helpful heart, the Rabbit and Rat produce the ultimate therapist to anyone in need. Anyone within this Rabbit's close group of trusted loved ones will have unfailing loyalty and support. She will enjoy working with others, thriving on teamwork and togetherness. This child will be an objective and deep thinker whom others will often seek for advice or consolation. On the other hand, the inquisitive Rat inner self is more calculating than the Rabbit. Both signs here love their security blanket and know how to take care of themselves as well as protect their own interests.

THE OX ASCENDANT—TIME OF BIRTH IS BETWEEN 1 A.M. AND 2:59 A.M.
This child will have more of a commanding presence than other Rabbits, with such a strong ascendant. The dutiful Ox as her inner self presents order and discipline to the fun-loving Rabbit, and this could be a combination destined for success. The strong Ox ascendant gives a more serious outlook to the agile Rabbit, who excels in interaction and mediation. The intuitive Rabbit side is skillful at communications and has great taste as well as good social graces—an excellent example of the iron fist in the velvet glove.

THE TIGER ASCENDANT—TIME OF BIRTH IS BETWEEN 3 A.M. AND 4:59 A.M.
In fast pursuit of the Tiger's adventures, this Rabbit will always be in motion. This bright child will be more outgoing than other Rabbits, but will maintain the poise and responsibility of the native sign. The Tiger ascendant will give the encouragement and confidence to follow through on what the Rabbit thinks are lofty ideas, but which the Tiger thinks can only be the beginning of greatness. This combination produces an optimistic child that will never say die and has the good sense of when to hold 'em and when to fold 'em. The Tiger inner

self gives fire and zest to the demure Rabbit personality, while the Rabbit side will be wise to follow its inborn intuition, not the Tiger's impulsiveness.

THE RABBIT ASCENDANT—TIME OF BIRTH IS BETWEEN 5 A.M. AND 6:59 A.M.

A double Rabbit sign is a sign of quiet wisdom and deep intellect. Always caught up in deep thought, this child could be a little philosopher in disguise. She has splendid instincts and very good and refined tastes. Although this child will always gravitate toward the finer things in life, she is the ultimate listener and poet, generous to others with her thoughts and advice. As a pure sign, she loves peace and calm, avoiding discomfort at all costs. This child is capable and clever in assessing situations and knows how to make the best of every circumstance. Her discriminating tastes and sense of style will be admired by all. A definite trendsetter with a dramatic flair!

THE DRAGON ASCENDANT—TIME OF BIRTH IS BETWEEN 7 A.M. AND 8:59 A.M.

The bold Dragon ascendant makes this child a leader who is able to bring out the best in others without much effort. Unlike some Rabbits, she will encourage others forcefully and could be straightforward about what she wants. With the Rabbit's soft touch, she will still be able to take advantage of the dynamic Dragon's gift of persuasion. This Rabbit will bring people together to get things done, rather than try to go at it alone or sulk quietly. The confidence of the Dragon inner self makes this Rabbit follow her ambitions with determination. This success-oriented child will achieve a lot while making friends and building harmonious bridges in life.

THE SNAKE ASCENDANT—TIME OF BIRTH IS BETWEEN 9 A.M. AND 10:59 A.M.

With the Snake as her inner self, this child will be passionate but fiercely private and even secretive. She tends to keep her counsel to herself and does not volunteer information unless asked. She might be the type to have many and different circles of friends, who often plays the listener and rarely confides in others. The Snake ascendant contributes a gift of perception in both environment and people. This tactful and enchanting child will be creative and resourceful in her own special way. When she asks for a favor, she will be so suave that it will be impossible to refuse her. She will find things that can be enjoyed independently, often in a private and quiet place. Very ambitious yet calm and unassuming, this child is a powerful combination destined to rise high and succeed at whatever she focuses on.

THE HORSE ASCENDANT—TIME OF BIRTH IS BETWEEN 11 A.M. AND 12:59 P.M.
The Horse ascendant combined with the Rabbit personality gives this child a confident and bubbly personality. The Horse inner self adds a special sort of self-esteem and adventurous spirit into the often bashful, introverted Rabbit. These two signs both have a sort of sixth sense when it comes to assessing situations that mystify everyone else. She will act on these hunches and run out and explore them without even a second thought. Quick, nimble, intelligent, and great at communications, the flamboyant Horse adds some spice to the flexible, even-tempered Rabbit. She rarely hesitates and is usually right in taking quick action.

THE SHEEP ASCENDANT—TIME OF BIRTH IS BETWEEN 1 P.M. AND 2:59 P.M.
The Sheep ascendant heightens the already creative talents of the Rabbit. She will have the gift of both discovering and creating art wherever she goes. Highly sensitive, this child may need extra support when developing her talents and hobbies. However, be gentle in guiding this child, as she has the soul of the artist and needs a great deal of reassurance and support. Sometimes, she may not be convinced that constructive criticism can be helpful, and she could be easily dismayed or discouraged by a lack of approval or enthusiasm. Understandably, such intense artistic talents combined with deep emotions may create an ultrasensitive child who sees life through rose-colored glasses.

THE MONKEY ASCENDANT—TIME OF BIRTH IS BETWEEN 3 P.M. AND 4:59 P.M.
This special child has the makings of the gifted inventor and wily strategist. A combination that matches the innovative Monkey's special gift of bending the rules with the discretion of the diplomatic Rabbit, this child can find ways of accomplishing anything and everything. The Monkey ascendant is an extro-verted inner self, which complements the reserved and sensitive Rabbit per-

sonality. Outgoing yet composed and creative, this charming Rabbit child will be able to make the most of whatever talents and special gifts she has with a quiet confidence and wonderful sense of humor and style.

THE ROOSTER ASCENDANT—TIME OF BIRTH IS BETWEEN 5 P.M. AND 6:59 P.M.
Intelligent and highly responsible, this composed Rabbit child receives the positive and negative traits of the Rooster ascendant. The two signs here are in conflict with each other and could produce a complicated personality that seeks perfection and harmony at the same time. The Rooster within encourages the modest Rabbit to be more outgoing, confident, and confrontational. This child will be intelligent and observant, and also independent and thoughtful. She will be someone who knows how to listen and how to speak forcefully when in command. Hopefully, the critical Rooster ascendant does not impede the Rabbit's need for consensus and cooperation in life. The Rabbit self may want to take the middle of the road and not offend anyone, if possible, but the Rooster enjoys splitting hairs and arguing instead of compromising.

THE DOG ASCENDANT—TIME OF BIRTH IS BETWEEN 7 P.M. AND 8:59 P.M.
You won't have to wait up for this child to come home. The Dog ascendant makes this Rabbit the model of responsibility and caution. She will surely be someone who follows through on her promises and will hate to let anyone down. The Rabbit's generosity finds a strong guardian in the Dog. This child will be confident, but not proud and controlling. The loyal Dog ascendant will make this Rabbit child less self-serving and more levelheaded. This child is not one to be influenced or manipulated, and nothing will change such a moral, upstanding person who knows how to bring out the best in both her friends and enemies. This child is a great mediator and peacemaker.

THE BOAR ASCENDANT—TIME OF BIRTH IS BETWEEN 9 P.M. AND 10:59 P.M.
The Boar ascendant merged with the debonair Rabbit personality could produce a socialite and philanthropist with a heart of gold. The life of the party, this sociable

child will be generous, smart, and accomplished in dealing with people. The Boar and the Rabbit combination creates a sparkling personality to which others will be drawn. She will have the gift of communication and can bring friends and foes together without any trouble at all. The Boar inner self provides this child with a special aura and abundant energy, which could liven up the conservative Rabbit.

Famous Persons Born in the Year of the Rabbit

Confucius	George Orwell
George C. Scott	Roger Moore
Queen Victoria	Eva Perón
Albert Einstein	David Frost
David Frost	Prince Albert
Edith Piaf	Harry Belafonte
King Bhumibol of Thailand	King Olav V of Norway
Henry Miller	Jomo Kenyatta
Orson Welles	David Rockefeller
Ingrid Bergman	Bob Hope
Marie Curie	Dr. Benjamin Spock
Lewis Carroll	Peter Falk
Gary Kasparov	Cary Grant
Fidel Castro	Tina Turner

As a treat to your child, please read the Rabbit's story,
"How the Rabbit Got to the Moon," which follows.

THE RABBIT'S STORY

"HOW THE RABBIT GOT TO THE MOON"

When the world was young and new, animals and humans and the immortals that lived in the heavens could talk to one another without much trouble at all. The Lord Emperor ruled the heavens, and all beneath the heavens were at peace.

This is the story of a beautiful Black Rabbit named Harmony. Harmony belonged to the renowned raven-colored tribe most valued for their astute sense of diplomacy and elegant manners. They had long upright ears and a sleek coat. The Black Hares were the largest and most imposing of all the Rabbits. Harmony had many cousins of different colors. The White Hares were noted for their fur, most commonly used for Chinese calligraphy brushes. The Red Hares had curly fur and floppy ears. The Blue, or Gray, Rabbits lived in the northern mountains and the Yellow, or Golden, Hares were smaller but faster than all the rest.

Harmony and her family and, in fact, all Rabbits were considered bearers of good news and were often employed to bring greetings from the immortals to humans or vice versa. They also carried messages from humans to humans. Since they always brought good news and even gifts, they were always a welcome sight. The speed and ability of the Hares to carry out their missions combined with their quiet grace and discretion was recognized and appreciated by all in Heaven and all under the heavens who valued their services.

Harmony was considered a very special news-bearing Rabbit, as she not only traveled fast but also knew many shortcuts, which she shared with all her friends. Well liked and respected, many of the other animals would seek Harmony out for her astute advice or ask for her opinions and interpretations on all manner of things. She was wise, yet kind and unassuming for her tender age, and knew all the rules and protocol of being a good courier.

Now, as I mentioned, the world was so very young that one day a catastrophe of immense proportions happened. Nine fiery suns emerged from what seemed like out of nowhere and decided to inhabit the heavens! The heat was tremendous, as one would imagine, and all the vegetation started to dry up and all under Heaven suffered greatly. The Lord Emperor of Heaven issued an edict challenging anyone to come up with a fast solution to remedy their terrible problem of having ten suns. Many tried to resolve this enormous problem, but they all failed. Then, an archer named Ho-Yi came forth and suggested that he could shoot down the rogue suns with magic arrows. But, the Lord Emperor said,

"Many have already tried to do what you suggest, but the suns are so high in the heavens that arrows do not reach them."

Ho-Yi nodded and replied, "Great Emperor of Heaven, I do not seek to shoot at the suns directly, but, rather, I shall go to the silver reflecting pool of the Queen Mother of Heaven and I shall shoot at the reflections of the suns instead."

Ho-Yi carried out his plan and as his magic arrows pierced the reflection of each sun, each melted away, leaving only one sun unharmed, as instructed by the Lord Emperor of Heaven. Once again, the sky was back to normal.

The world was saved by Ho-Yi and everyone was so grateful that the archer became a famous hero overnight. The Lord Emperor decided to reward Ho-Yi by asking the Queen Mother to give Ho-Yi a Pearl of Immortality. When he swallowed the pearl, Ho-Yi would become immortal and he would be able to become a heavenly warrior and protect both mankind and the immortals. Of course, Ho-Yi was very pleased with this great honor, but since he had befriended the Queen Mother herself, he confided his true feelings to her kind majesty.

"I lead a lonely life and my happiness would be complete if I could find someone to share my life with me."

"Say no more, I understand," replied the Queen Mother. "We must correct the situation and find you a suitable wife immediately!"

So the Queen Mother gathered the loveliest ladies of the realm and Ho-Yi chose the beautiful Chang-O to be his bride. Chang-O was indeed lovely, but she was also vain and selfish. She wanted to marry Ho-Yi because he was famous and would be extremely rich—not to mention immortal, after he received the Pearl of Immortality from the Queen Mother of Heaven.

After the wedding of Ho-Yi and Chang-O, the Queen Mother thought things over and decided that as a wedding gift, she would bestow two pearls for the newlyweds instead of only one for her favorite, Ho-Yi, the archer. She wrapped her gifts in a special imperial jade pouch and summoned a Black Hare to deliver the gift. Harmony was chosen as the royal courier for this mission. The scroll of congratulations and the jade pouch with the two pearls were tied around Harmony's neck as she set off posthaste to the mansion of the now Lord Ho-Yi and Lady Chang-O.

When Harmony arrived, Lady Chang-O received her and took the scroll as well as the pouch at once.

"Where is the Lord Ho-Yi?" asked Harmony politely. "I was instructed by the Queen Mother to deliver the pouch and the scroll directly to him."

"My husband is asleep and cannot be disturbed. He had a hard day and must get some rest. As his lady wife, I thank you for delivering this gift. Do not be concerned. Everything is safe in my care. You may go." And Lady Chang-O dismissed Harmony with a wave of her hand.

Harmony left the mansion but had some misgivings, so she waited outside the front door to see if Ho-Yi would awaken soon and send back a message of thanks to the Queen Mother, which his wife had so rudely neglected to do in a proper and courtly manner. Chang-O, in the meantime, had read the scroll and opened the pouch. She now knew that one of the pearls was meant for her and she was delighted. Eagerly, she swallowed the pearl and began to feel light and a bit dizzy. Then, she clutched the other pearl and was about to awaken Ho-Yi with the wonderful news when she thought to herself:

"Why should Ho-Yi become an immortal? I should keep the second pearl for someone I feel would be more deserving. I do not love Ho-Yi and the idea of spending an eternity with this rough, uncouth warrior is more than I can bear."

So, Chang-O decided to slip out of the mansion and run away before Ho-Yi woke up and found out what happened. As Chang-O opened the door to leave, she looked back and tripped on a step of the entrance and fell right on top of Harmony. As fate would have it, Chang-O dropped the second pearl when she stumbled and it fell straight into the surprised Harmony's agape mouth. Harmony swallowed the second pearl without meaning to and so became immortal. When the Lady Chang-O realized what happened, she became extremely angry with the Rabbit and tried to choke Harmony and force her to spit up the pearl. It was then that both Chang-O and Harmony discovered that they felt light because besides immortality, the pearl had also given them the power of flight. As they both floated up into the sky with Chang-O screaming and choking the innocent Harmony, Ho-Yi awoke and went to investigate the commotion outside his home.

Quickly, Chang-O clutched Harmony and flew even higher. Later, she and the hapless Rabbit hid in a large cave to evade an angry Ho-Yi, who had found out that his faithless wife had taken off with the pearl that was intended for him. The Queen Mother was duly informed of what the treacherous Chang-O did and she sought a way to punish Chang-O. Yet the Queen Mother did not believe in vengeance and would not allow Ho-Yi to pursue his wife further or harm her. As the world was so very young then, no one had inhabited the moon, so the Queen Mother banished the Lady Chang-O to the moon. She also asked Harmony, who had gained immortality quite by accident, if she would agree to go with Chang-O, take up residence there, and watch over the vain lady to make sure she thought about what she had done. Harmony gladly obliged the Queen Mother's wishes and offered her services selflessly. Besides, the moon was a most beautiful and peaceful place.

During a full moon, we can see Harmony standing under a very large, old cassia tree with flowing, cloudlike branches. The cassia tree is known as a symbol of forgiveness. One is not able to see Lady Chang-O next to Harmony in the moon, because it is believed that her vanity, anger, and selfishness turned her into a toad and she sits on a rock beneath the large Black Rabbit. The benevolent Queen Mother had instructed that Chang-O could be released when she showed remorse and begged forgiveness for what she had done. But, to this day, the unrepentant Chang-O has refused.

Thousands of years passed and the Chinese people grew to love the fabled Moon Hare. The Rabbit became a symbol of fertility and the patron saint of women who wanted to conceive a baby. As they gazed at Harmony during a full moon, their wishes for a child were often answered.

CHAPTER FIVE

THE DRAGON

The Fifth Lunar Sign

The Dragon is the visionary

Of the lunar zodiac.

At the center of everything—

He exudes energy and optimism and is

Blessed with a big and brave heart.

A dynamic and positive leader,

He is capable and hardworking—

Always willing to sacrifice.

He seeks to accomplish the

Impossible, try the untried.

One cannot help but be drawn

To the magnetic and magnificent Dragon.

His motto is: **THE HEAVIEST LOAD IN LIFE
IS NOT HAVING ANYTHING TO CARRY**

THE DRAGON'S BRANCH

CHINESE NAME FOR THE DRAGON: *Long*

RANK: Fifth

HOURS OF THE DRAGON: From 7 A.M. to 8:59 A.M.*

DIRECTION OF THIS BRANCH: East-southeast

SEASON AND PRINCIPAL MONTH: Spring and April

CORRESPONDS TO THE WESTERN SIGN: Aries, the Ram

FIXED ELEMENT: Wood

STEM: Yang, or masculine

*Ascendant: *Children who are born during the two-hour segment of the day ruled by the Dragon sign will have this sign as their ascendant and will display affinity for people born under this particular sign, as well as have many of the distinct character traits that identify the Dragon sign.*

FIVE CYCLES* OF THE LUNAR YEARS OF THE DRAGON IN THE WESTERN CALENDAR

START DATE		END DATE	ELEMENT OF THE YEAR
February 13, 1964	to	February 1, 1965	Wood
January 31, 1976	to	February 17, 1977	Fire
February 17, 1988	to	February 5, 1989	Earth
February 5, 2000	to	January 23, 2001	Metal
January 23, 2012	to	February 9, 2013	Water

* A cycle on the lunar horoscope equals twelve years. Five cycles completes sixty years.

Note: One who is born on the day before the start of the lunar year of the Dragon, e.g., February 4, 2000, will belong to the animal sign before the Dragon, which is the Rabbit, the fourth lunar sign. One who is born on the day after the end of the lunar year of the Dragon, e.g., January 24, 2001, will belong to the animal sign following the Dragon, which is the Snake, the sixth lunar sign.

龍

無責沉逾挑重担

克昌題

美秀畫

THE DRAGON SIGN

THE HEAVIEST LOAD IN LIFE IS NOT HAVING ANYTHING TO CARRY

The Dragon Personality

The fifth earth branch of the Chinese lunar cycle is that of the Dragon. In Chinese, this fifth sign is known as the *Chen* branch. A child born with the *Chen* personality is known for his love of action, vitality, positive attitude, and unifying leadership. The upbeat Dragon is always the first to volunteer, the first to help, and the first to speak out. This personality feels duty bound to fulfill all responsibilities thrust upon him. He holds himself accountable for all the obligations and promises he takes on and will always do his best never to disappoint those he loves. He won't let you down, not if he can help it.

The Dragon child is drawn to challenges with optimism and fearlessness. If properly motivated, he can accomplish much and overcome all sorts of oppositions and setbacks in life. Confident in his own abilities and forthright in everything he does, the Dragon child is idealistic and purposeful. He has unquestioning faith in his parents and tends to put them up on a pedestal. This child develops strong convictions early in life and is most in need of good role models and mentors to guide and show him the way.

Action oriented, the Dragon child enjoys group activities and entertainment. He shines when he is able to prove himself worthy of responsibility and trust. Because the Dragon child is very impressionable, he could easily become fanatical in his devotion to special causes or persons he becomes attached to. He doesn't back out or back down from a fight and will not give up easily. At times, he can be overzealous and unreasonable. This child can also be aggressive and controlling because he is so intense in what he believes in. He could become self-centered and opinionated if not taught to control his strong impulses. With him, it's never having too much to do, but rather not enough. However, he must learn early in life that might is not right, or he may intimidate others to do his will without even being aware of it.

The formidable Dragon child should be taught to curb his egotism and inspire others to work with him through the power of persuasion and goodwill. If he is able to polish his social skills, he may grow to be a natural leader who will achieve his goals magnificently.

When he agrees to do something, it is usually with total commitment. The enthusiastic Dragon child does not work in half measures and is never lazy or unmotivated. At school, he could be impatient and intolerant when others fail to do what they are supposed to or break promises to him. He can be outspoken and self-righteous and is never afraid to give his opinion.

Ambitious and single-minded, the Dragon child loves his parents, reveres his teachers, and is always protective of his friends. He has an army of supporters and loyal friends. He has a bold yet compassionate heart, which matches his strength of character and buoyant spirit. The Dragon child of the fifth branch has enormous willpower that will serve him well in life. His faith in himself will carry him through difficulties and defeat. His is the sign of the idealistic visionary who could make all his dreams come true with his dedication and magnetism.

Birth Order and Sibling Rivalry

*FIRSTBORN OR ONLY CHILD

A Dragon child in the position of the firstborn or only child is destined to become an overachiever. In Chinese mythology, the Dragon wears the "horns of destiny" and is always given a position of honor because he works hard to earn recognition. Likewise, this child will always want to be number one in his parents' eyes. Of course, as the firstborn or only child, the Dragon personality is fiercely competitive and not at all shy about what he wants. He can be very demanding and forceful when he thinks he is entitled to something. However, he is not afraid of hard work or serious commitment and will apply himself happily to finishing tasks that are handed to him. Not one to complain or feel sorry for himself, the Dragon child is great as a role model for the younger siblings. His siblings will be inspired by the Dragon's leadership and devotion to

* When a child is born five years after another child, he or she is also considered a firstborn child.

duty. On the other hand, he could have a strong temper and will not suffer insubordination of any kind.

MIDDLE OR LATER-BORN CHILD

When the Dragon child is the second or later-born child, he is a great pillar of strength and reliability. This is because he is ready to step into the firstborn's shoes anytime he finds him lacking and remiss in his duties. This need to dethrone the firstborn is what motivates the Dragon child who is only second in line to the crown. But, he still considers himself better equipped to carry out the duties of being first and finds it quite unfair that he has to listen to the first-born. However, if the older sibling is comfortable in his role as the leader of the pack, the Dragon who is in the middle will learn to cooperate. Yet the Dragon is always straining on the leash to rush ahead and show his talents. This is an aggressive and confident child who needs challenges and recognition. He is competent and knows how to manage and market himself well.

YOUNGEST OR LAST-BORN CHILD

As the youngest, this Dragon child will mature early and try to imitate the older ones by being serious and funny at the same time. A charming and very intelligent child, he will know how to bring people together, with himself in the limelight, of course. In this position, the Dragon will master the art of manipulating his parents and older siblings. His teachers and peers will marvel at his popularity and social graces. However, underneath all that charm and persuasiveness still lies a strong willpower and determination that is the Dragon's fire. He may be deceptively quiet or loud and domineering, but he does know what he wants and, more important, knows how to get it.

Ascendants

In Chinese horoscopes, the two-hour segment ruling the time of birth is known as the ascendant sign. This can also be referred to as the child's "inner self."

The time of birth used to determine the ascendant is always the local time in the place of birth.

For a child born in the Year of the Dragon:

THE RAT ASCENDANT—TIME OF BIRTH IS BETWEEN 11 P.M. AND 12:59 A.M.
This child will have both the open heart of the Dragon and the Rat's sensibility to play gatekeeper to that big heart. The Dragon mind communicates simply and honestly. But, the crafty inner self of the Rat can find more and better opportunities for the illustrious Dragon to apply himself. The result in this child will be a Dragon who can persuade with charm and warmth and is not as confrontational or openly bold as other Dragons. With the Rat as his ascendant, this Dragon is not only hardworking but has a great way with words and will be an astute writer.

THE OX ASCENDANT—TIME OF BIRTH IS BETWEEN 1 A.M. AND 2:59 A.M.
With the determined Ox ascendant as his inner self, this child will be able to accomplish anything he feels strongly about. At times, the busy schedule of this multitasking Dragon may seem impossible, but he will surely accomplish everything on the list. The dedicated Ox steadies the fiery and often unpredictable Dragon. Hopefully, the practical Ox will be able to keep the Dragon's feet on the ground with his down-to-earth outlook. Nevertheless, the fire of the idealistic Dragon is never quenched. He just may be better able to focus and direct his energy with the Ox's stable influence and guidance.

THE TIGER ASCENDANT—TIME OF BIRTH IS BETWEEN 3 A.M. AND 4:59 A.M.
A born do-gooder, this irrepressible child possesses a strong and generous heart. He is unfailingly loyal yet a bit unpredictable. The Tiger and Dragon create a person who will always fight the good fight and never forget any friendship that is genuine. Indeed, he will be a valuable resource. This child will have big dreams, but must learn the difference between the dreamscape and the world that the rest

of us live in. The impulsive Tiger ascendant brings a good deal of excitement into the Dragon's idealism and need to perform great things. These two signs produce a very strong and magnetic personality, although unpredictable.

THE RABBIT ASCENDANT—TIME OF BIRTH IS BETWEEN 5 A.M. AND 6:59 A.M.
This child will exude a capable yet composed personality that brings together one and all. The Rabbit contributes an objective and thoughtful demeanor. Unlike other Dragons, this one will score high marks with all kinds of people and know when to hold his tongue. He will undoubtedly be very social and no doubt be the main attraction at any social get-together. This kind of charisma and skill will ensure great success in many endeavors for this loveable child. The Rabbit ascendant brings harmony into the Dragon's need to dominate and finds other ways to win without actually having a fight or contest.

THE DRAGON ASCENDANT—TIME OF BIRTH IS BETWEEN 7 A.M. AND 8:59 A.M.
The double punch of the Dragon sign delivers energy and spectacular fireworks. All eyes will be on this kid, much to his liking. Classmates and strangers will find this child irresistible yet quite intimidating at times. A double Dragon is not a personality to be taken lightly, or easily forgotten, for that matter. Peers and classmates will either love or hate this powerful Dragon personality, but, no matter, he still forges on relentlessly toward the destiny he has chosen for himself. With his inner strength and self-confidence, this child will be the ultimate go-getter.

THE SNAKE ASCENDANT—TIME OF BIRTH IS BETWEEN 9 A.M. AND 10:59 A.M.
The Snake ascendant provides the Dragon with the wisdom to keep his ambitions a secret. Here the combined talents of the Snake and the Dragon produce a mesmerizing personality who will not strike until everything is ready and in place. Like most Dragons, this child will have a knack for conversation and great ease with initiating relationships. The Dragon-Snake child has a tendency to be more guarded than others, but should still have that Snake charisma that is so

attractive. If this child can direct his focus and use the Dragon's strength as a base, his natural confidence and intuition will certainly take him far.

THE HORSE ASCENDANT—TIME OF BIRTH IS BETWEEN 11 A.M. AND 12:59 P.M.

The passionate Horse ascendant creates a Dragon child that can feel the full extreme of emotions. Adventurous, happy-go-lucky, and action oriented, he is always on the go. With the popular Horse as his inner self, this confident Dragon child will not hesitate to take risks and may have to be cautioned to be less adventurous. A superb leader, he will never ask anyone to do anything he can't do and probably will be competitive to the limit in sports and all academic activity. If one can curb this tendency to spontaneous flight, this Dragon will certainly benefit from the surefooted Horse. This free spirit has a positive attitude that will be quite bright and clever, although unpredictable.

THE SHEEP ASCENDANT—TIME OF BIRTH IS BETWEEN 1 P.M. AND 2:59 P.M.

A model citizen with a genuine heart, the Sheep ascendant lends thoughtfulness, grace, and softness to the dynamic Dragon child. With the tolerant and good-hearted Sheep as his inner self, he loves to help others, while the Dragon half is an expert in judging character, which makes for someone that can definitely pick his friends and allies. Together with the Dragon's natural charm, the kind Sheep ascendant is a lovely complement to an already irresistible personality. Here is a Dragon that is not so controlling or demanding. Still, he is able to achieve his goals in an agreeable and cooperative way.

THE MONKEY ASCENDANT—TIME OF BIRTH IS BETWEEN 3 P.M. AND 4:59 P.M.

The Monkey ascendant brings two of the keenest signs in the zodiac together. The world has big plans for this child. He will be a natural entertainer and seek out challenges to showcase his talents. This child will be creative, resourceful, and a wizard at making connections. Tough to figure out at times, he will be able to project images and cast spells on a whim. One should never underestimate this formidable combination; what this child guards within is powerful indeed. The brainy Monkey brings in strategy and helps the Dragon self figure out things before charging ahead. A calculating Dragon who is motivated but knows how to play the game to his own advantage—always!

THE ROOSTER ASCENDANT—TIME OF BIRTH IS BETWEEN 5 P.M. AND 6:59 P.M.
With the Rooster as his ascendant, this child will be confident and creative, one who sticks to his dreams and never says die. The diligent Rooster provides a strong work ethic that will enable the Dragon's lofty aspirations to come true. Others will be sure to take notice of such responsibility and resourcefulness. The flamboyant Rooster and the powerful Dragon create a person who will enjoy debate and controversy and is gifted with energy and good stamina. It would be hard to outwork or outtalk him. He can be set in his ways, and although he likes to present himself as a shining example, he can be opinioned and stuck on his own views. He does respect authority and is obedient to the letter. Not one to stray from the righteous path, he still has big dreams or grand plans and does not like to take advice or hear anything contrary to what he wants.

THE DOG ASCENDANT—TIME OF BIRTH IS BETWEEN 7 P.M. AND 8:59 P.M.
The loyalty of the Dog ascendant makes this child the champion crusader of all those in need. His kindness and compassion will be apparent to anyone that comes into contact with this warm and likeable child. He will seek out opportunities to help others and try to better the world with typical Dragon largesse, with himself at the helm, of course. Champion of justice and fairness, this remarkable child never hesitates to speak out and defend his beliefs against all odds. Thankfully, with the Dog as his inner self, this Dragon child is never overoptimistic or very egotistic. The sensible Dog ascendant provides a good balance for the zealous and enthusiastic Dragon personality.

THE BOAR ASCENDANT—TIME OF BIRTH IS BETWEEN 9 P.M. AND 10:59 P.M.
A natural leader and trendsetter, this Dragon child will be able to rally friends, family, and perfect strangers to his battle call with the Boar as his ascendant. He

might have a knack for public speaking or for the written word, with such strong emotions, social skills, and vision. The Boar influences the Dragon's appetite for life's sweet treats and can often lose control when confronted with tempting offers. With a tendency to bite off more than he can chew, this Dragon might need to learn discipline and sacrifice and curb his indulgences. With the Boar as his inner self, this Dragon loves passionately and will give totally of himself. Devoted to family and friends, he is always ready to lend a helping hand and put in a good word.

Famous Persons Born in the Year of the Dragon

King Constantine II of Greece	Queen Margrethe II of Denmark
John Lennon	Placido Domingo
Jimmy Connors	St. Joan of Arc
St. Bernadette	Haile Selassie
Mae West	Bing Crosby
Betty Grable	Sir Edward Heath
Florence Nightingale	Frank Sinatra
Yehudi Menuhin	Harold Wilson
Ernesto "Che" Guevara	Walter Mondale
Shirley Temple Black	Salvador Dali
Deng Xiaoping	François Mitterrand

As a treat to your child, please read the Dragon's story,
"Why Dragons Celebrate Chinese New Year," which follows.

THE DRAGON'S STORY

"WHY DRAGONS CELEBRATE CHINESE NEW YEAR"

Many thousands and thousands of years ago, when the world was very young, the mighty Dragons roamed the waters and the land. In the winter, they slept as stone formations atop the hills, to be awakened on the first day of spring by the swarming of the insects. They would rise and play in the rain and dance together, soaring way up into the sky. During the summer storms and thundershowers, the Dragons would climb up into the heavens and play all sorts of games, such as hide-and-seek in the clouds, to test their other awesome powers.

One of the very beautiful and wise mother Dragons had a little Dragon son called Yu Ling (which means "rain in the forest"). Yu Ling was very curious about the humans who lived in the lowlands, especially the Chinese peasants who were happy, noisy, and also a hardworking lot. Yu Ling would sneak away from his mother to go and watch the Chinese farmers from a distance, working in the fields, fishing in the streams, or herding the farm animals.

One day, he did not find anyone in the fields, so he went over to the ponds to see if anyone was fishing, but he only saw the ducks swimming and diving and shaking their tails. Then, Yu Ling heard drums banging and popping sounds coming from the Town Square. He had never gone into the center of the town, as his mother told him to be careful of humans. But Yu Ling was compelled by curiosity and went further into the town to investigate. It looked like the humans were having a large celebration. This was the first time that Yu Ling saw that the farmers were enjoying themselves. This was also the first time he saw them set off red and green firecrackers that were strung together and went off like rolling thunder. When he ran to his mother to tell her about what he saw, she explained that the humans were easily frightened and would light firecrackers to scare off anything they thought was evil or dangerous with

the exploding sounds. They also believed that loud noise would drive away any bad luck or unwanted intruders.

"Naturally, those firecrackers cannot possibly hurt us," said his mother, "but we stay away in order avoid any trouble. Humans are humans and Dragons are Dragons, my son."

"But, Mother, I like those noisy firecrackers and drums and all that dancing and jumping around. You should have seen the acrobats leap and build human towers in their bright silk clothes!" said the little Dragon. "Couldn't I just watch from up in the trees where they won't see me?"

Yu Ling had emerald green scales like his mother and blended beautifully in the large trees and bamboo groves.

His mother let out a long Dragon sigh with puffs of smoke to show her disapproval, but she was too wise to actually forbid her child from watching the humans. To do so would just encourage the young one to rebel. She knew he was just a happy but very active and curious Dragon child.

"Well, I guess you may," she replied, "but I think you should spend more time with your young Dragon friends instead of hanging around the humans."

Dragons live a long time, some say forever. And when they are ready to die, if they really do, they simply lie in their favorite place and turn into stone. That is why there are so many Dragon-shaped rocks on hills and mountains, and Dragon-shaped boulders in rivers and streams and even in caves.

For young Yu Ling, it took a number of years before he got closer and closer to the village. He loved the way the humans worked and played, but most of all, he loved the sound of their laughter. After some years, he even began to understand what they were saying to each other.

A decade went by before Yu Ling felt comfortable camping up on a large mulberry tree behind the old temple. There he could get a bird's-eye view of the entire village and all the little houses that surrounded the Town Square. But, he always left when the first snow fell to join his mother and fellow Dragons to sleep until the spring.

But one year, winter was late in arriving and Yu Ling stayed longer than he had ever done. His mother and the rest of the Dragon clan had already gone to sleep by the time he returned to the hills, and Yu Ling realized that he was the only Dragon still awake.

"I've never stayed awake in winter," he thought to himself. "I wonder what the humans do during this time of cold and snow."

Yu Ling decided to creep back to his hideout and spend the winter near the village. Sleep was a waste of time, since Dragons were not affected by heat or cold and really did not need rest. It was just something they all did in the wintertime. His mother called it "tradition."

A quiet two weeks went by before Yu Ling saw more activity. The humans were busy cleaning their homes, pasting red papers with gold drawings on their doors, and hanging bright lanterns and banners all around. They even built a huge canopy over the whole Town Square and set up a big stage in the middle. Everything was scrubbed clean and looked new. The wonderful smell of cooking filled the air. But best of all, bundles and bundles of stringed firecrackers dangled from windows and doors all around town.

"Ah, they are going to have a really big festival," said Yu Ling to himself. "How wonderful. I would have missed it all if I had gone back to the mountains to sleep this year."

Finally, on the eve of a dazzling New Moon, all the humans stayed up way past their bedtime to feast and wish each other a Happy Chinese New Year. Children wore red and gold outfits and ran about bowing to everyone who gave them treats and red envelopes. The temple and altars were cleaned and filled with offerings. Incense smoke filled the air as everyone rushed around celebrating the coming of the lunar New Year.

After dinner, the crowd gathered around the Town Square to watch the drummers and musicians bang their cymbals. The acrobats showed their skills and everyone clapped happily to cheer them on. Yu Ling became so wrapped up himself that he did not realize that he had crept down from his hiding place. He was so caught up in the celebrations that he decided to join in the fun.

Imagine the crowd's surprise when a beautiful young emerald green Dragon jumped onto the stage and began to dance. If there's anything Dragons do well, it's dance. They have a lot of practice riding the storm and dancing in the rain. Yu Ling did a spectacular Dragon Dance. He bopped and swayed, thumped his feet, and waved his tail in magnificent Dragon style.

At first, everyone was stunned speechless. But then they realized their good fortune at being visited by a real, live Dragon and they oohed and aahed in wonderment. It was time to light the firecrackers as the midnight hour arrived, so Yu Ling started another dance to ward off evil spirits and bad, mischievous demons from the village. The humans joined in as they formed a chain, with Yu Ling taking the lead, weaving around the square. Everyone had a wonderful time and laughed and sang all through the night. They bowed deeply to the young Dragon and they all agreed it was a very good and lucky sign to have his presence at their celebrations.

Soon the news traveled throughout the Middle Kingdom (as China was called in those days) and everyone from the emperor to the poorest peasant celebrated Chinese New Year with a dancing Dragon to bring good luck to all.

Of course, they could not have a real Dragon like Yu Ling visit them, so they made a gigantic Dragon head out of paper and cloth and fashioned a long, streaming Dragon body and tail with bright scales. They would all hide under the head and Dragon body, which could fit many people, and they would do the Dragon Dance round and round the Town Square to welcome in the New Year. Before the dance, it also became a tradition to have the mayor or most important person in town dot the eyes of the paper Dragon with red ink to bring the Dragon to life.

After many, many years of visiting the humans, Yu Ling finally decided to return to his mother in the mountains and tell all his Dragon family and friends stories about how the humans lived and played and celebrated Chinese New Year. His fellow Dragons enjoyed Yu Ling's stories and continued to live their happy, boisterous life in the sky, where they were lords and masters of the thunder and rains. And, no doubt, during the summer thunderstorms, you can almost still hear them doing the Dragon Dance up in the clouds.

CHAPTER SIX

THE SNAKE

The Sixth Lunar Sign

The realistic Snake personality is the

Strategist of the twelve earth branches.

Wise and charismatic,

She is gifted with a deep abiding

Faith in herself—

And a constancy of purpose.

Unwavering in her focus,

Dedicated and patient,

She can outwait, outlast, and outwit

Her opponents.

The Snake is a master of tenacity.

Her motto is: **WAIT LONG, STRIKE FAST!**

THE SNAKE'S BRANCH

CHINESE NAME FOR THE SNAKE: *Shé*

RANK: Sixth

HOURS OF THE SNAKE: From 9 A.M. to 10:59 A.M.*

DIRECTION OF THIS BRANCH: South-southeast

SEASON AND PRINCIPAL MONTH: Spring and May

CORRESPONDS TO THE WESTERN SIGN: Taurus, the Bull

FIXED ELEMENT: Fire

STEM: Yin, or feminine

* Ascendant: *Children who are born during the two-hour segment of the day ruled by the Snake sign will have this sign as their ascendant and will display affinity for people born under this particular sign, as well as have many of the distinct character traits that identify the Snake sign.*

FIVE CYCLES* OF THE LUNAR YEARS OF THE SNAKE IN THE WESTERN CALENDAR

START DATE		END DATE	ELEMENT OF THE YEAR
February 2, 1965	to	January 20, 1966	Wood
February 18, 1977	to	February 6, 1978	Fire
February 6, 1989	to	January 26, 1990	Earth
January 24, 2001	to	February 11, 2002	Metal
February 10, 2013	to	January 30, 2014	Metal

* A cycle on the lunar horoscope equals twelve years. Five cycles completes sixty years.

Note: One who is born on the day before the start of the lunar year of the Snake, e.g., January 23, 2001, will belong to the animal sign before the Snake, which is the Dragon, the fifth lunar sign. One who is born on the day after the end of the lunar year of the Snake, e.g., February 12, 2002, will belong to the animal sign following the Snake, which is the Horse, the seventh lunar sign.

蛇

久察迅奪

克昌題

美秀畫

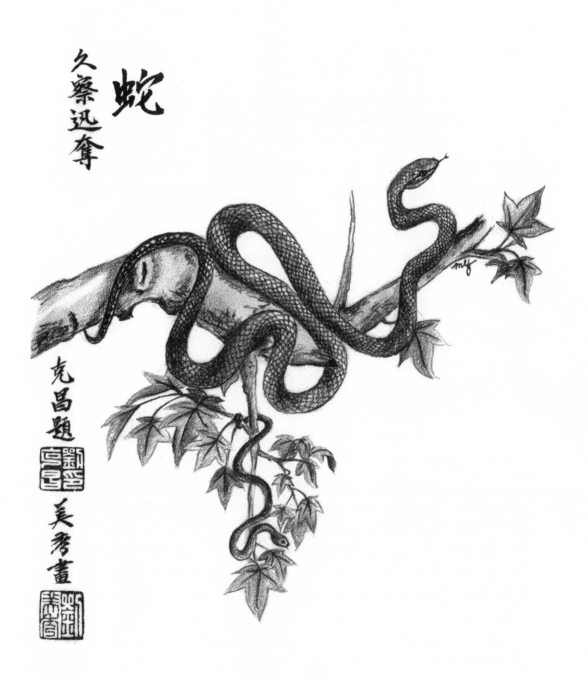

THE SNAKE SIGN
WAIT LONG, STRIKE FAST

The Snake Personality

The sixth lunar sign of the Chinese zodiac is the Snake. This corresponds to the *Si* earth branch, and this personality is renowned for her strength, stamina, and wisdom. The *Si* native is known for being calm, cool, and collected, even under pressure, yet simmering with resolve and ambition. Likewise, a child born under this auspicious sign is going to be purposeful and resolute in her approach to life.

The Snake child tends to be possessive of her parents and loved ones. She does not want to let go of anyone or anything that she becomes attached to. She may appear aloof, uncaring, and even disinterested, but in reality she cares deeply about being in control of her environment and how she could influence the turn of events around her. Despite her charming and personable demeanor, the Snake child is a thinker. She likes to plot her moves in advance and tends to plan and organize her life carefully. A worrier, she does not enjoy surprises, even happy ones, and can be quite vigilant and sometimes pessimistic in her outlook, especially when she feels others may not live up to her expectations. But then again, she does expect a lot from others; even when she does not say it, you may see the disappointment in her eyes.

The Snake has great faith in her own abilities and does not hesitate to grab opportunities when they come her way. However, although others do look up to her, she does not make a good leader, as she tends to be secretive and suspicious, although she does not openly show it. Being a strategist at heart, she is constantly weighing the pros and cons and cannot help but distrust others and suspect their motives when she is feeling negative. Because her mind works in a very complicated way, it is hard to fully understand how incredibly focused and intense a Snake child can be when she sets her mind to achieve something. Nothing will deter her from her goal.

The Snake rarely cares to explain her reasons or motives. Her only responsibility is to herself, and she does not feel that she needs confirmation or validation from others. If she is close to her parents and bonds early, she will take them into her inner sanctum and value their advice and support. Otherwise, she could become an introvert who is realistic and able to reflect on issues by herself, making careful judgments after studying and verifying all the facts to her satisfaction.

The Snake child matures early because of her serious outlook and intellectual superiority. On the surface, she may have a cheerful and outgoing disposition, but she is usually driven by her ambitions and deep convictions. She can be harsh and vindictive to her enemies and will show no mercy when she is crossed. She can wait forever to get even and has a long memory if anyone wrongs her.

The Snake child is known for her staying power. She knows how to conserve her resources and is a master of endurance. Her coping skills and patience are great, and she will wear you out with her persistence until you agree to give in. The Snake's shrewdness can be seen in her ability to assess situations and her likely chances for success if she pursues a certain goal or takes a different path. Her perseverance is quite remarkable, as she rarely loses sight of her objective.

The refined Snake child loves her privacy and will tend to withdraw inward if anyone tries to pry. On the other hand, she does respect the privacy of others and shows her thoughtfulness and consideration in many ways. She rarely takes things for granted or assumes that something is a "done deal." The Snake tends to be nervous, although she presents a very serene outer appearance. She needs permanence and security, and this is why she looks for ways to mold and control her environment and those around her.

The Snake child is deliberate in her approach. She recognizes her own abilities and establishes value early, and she tends to gravitate toward the finer things in life. The Snake child will be voted most likely to succeed and she will indeed make her mark in the world based on her own merit and abilities.

Birth Order and Sibling Rivalry

*FIRSTBORN OR ONLY CHILD

The Snake child in this position understands the power she holds over her parents and siblings. And don't think for one moment she does not know how to use it. As the firstborn, she rules supreme and is quite aware of how others should listen to her. An overachiever with a tendency to dwell on issues until they get resolved, the Snake child as the firstborn or only child is an efficient and very determined go-getter. Never content to be only the first, she will also want to be the best. At times, she acknowledges her younger siblings as though they were her loyal subjects, and she expects them to rally around her and support her on all her projects. She can be very generous and caring when she feels that everyone is part of her team.

MIDDLE OR LATER-BORN CHILD

The second or middle child born under the sign of the Snake is more laid back. She is quite comfortable, as she knows who she is and what she wants. She will figure out early in life that it is not to her advantage to compete with the first-born. Rather, she will establish her own elite circle of friends and work to achieve her goals independently. If she is shrewd, this child will conceal her ambitions until she is ready to strike, and she will do so without hesitation. Because of her well-mannered and calm disposition, her parents will value her opinion and connections. The middle position suits the Snake well, as she is a cautious observer who would rather sit and wait for the opportunities to come to her than go out and grab the bull by the horns. This Snake child is protective of the younger siblings and will look out for their welfare.

YOUNGEST OR LAST-BORN CHILD

Wise and enchanting in a bright and attractive way, the Snake child in this birth position is well regarded by all in the family. She is careful not to overstep

---

* When a child is born five years after another child, he or she is also considered a firstborn child.

bounds and does not openly challenge the other siblings. Why should she, when she could get them to do her bidding in other ways? This could be the most controlling of the Snake children, yet you will never know it. Still waters run deep, and at times, the Snake as the youngest runs very deep and profound in her outlook. Her confidence and faith in herself is endearing to her parents and they rarely doubt that she will do as she plans, for in spite of being the "baby" she is more than able to take care of herself.

Ascendants

In Chinese horoscopes, the two-hour segment ruling the time of birth is known as the ascendant sign. This can also be referred to as the child's "inner self."

The time of birth used to determine the ascendant is always the local time in the place of birth.

For a child born in the Year of the Snake:

THE RAT ASCENDANT—TIME OF BIRTH IS BETWEEN 11 P.M. AND 12:59 A.M.
With the Rat as her ascendant, this child knows how to make friends as well as keep a secret. This elegant Snake child will possess tenacity combined with shrewdness and resourcefulness. Charming and popular, she is able to get information when and where she wants, and her circle of friends only widens as she ages. She will keep friends and family close, sometimes too close, as she may be sentimental and possessive of these people. These tight relationships create strong attachments but also make for tough good-byes. She will be very caring of her parents and is thoughtful and considerate of their welfare.

THE OX ASCENDANT—TIME OF BIRTH IS BETWEEN 1 A.M. AND 2:59 A.M.
This ascendant creates a more generous Snake child who is also strong-willed and stubborn. The Ox ascendant makes this child more of an introvert who is very objective and decisive. Both signs here are contemplative and love privacy,

but she will feel a natural responsibility to look out for others and be a strong pillar of support for her family. Realistic and dependable, this ambitious child builds enduring relationships and knows exactly what she wants in life. She will certainly get it with her strength and stamina.

THE TIGER ASCENDANT—TIME OF BIRTH IS BETWEEN 3 A.M. AND 4:59 A.M.
Strongly passionate and articulate, this Snake child will communicate her feelings very openly. The Tiger ascendant brings out the natural entertainer of this young Snake, who will have a rather unique sense of humor. Her moods could swing to extremes with the vivacious Tiger ascendant, and although she is bright and captivating, she could also be volatile and jealous when she is not the center of attention. If this Snake child is able to control the Tiger's impulses and quick tongue and remain coolheaded, she will go far and achieve her ambitions with her innate Snake intuition.

THE RABBIT ASCENDANT—TIME OF BIRTH IS BETWEEN 5 A.M. AND 6:59 A.M.
This child is blessed by the Rabbit's accurate intuition watching over her. This ascendant also contributes an easygoing, peaceful attitude, which encourages taking advantage of life's just desserts. This charismatic Snake child still knows how to come out of any situation on top, and the Rabbit ascendant is a worthy accomplice. Others would be wise not to pull any fast ones on this kid. Yet she is always polite, sincere, observant, and, above all, discreet and sensitive to the feelings of others. She enjoys the arts tremendously and shares a love of music, art, and literature with her parents. She will probably pursue a career rich in any artistic talents that she may possess.

THE DRAGON ASCENDANT—TIME OF BIRTH IS BETWEEN 7 A.M. AND 8:59 A.M.
Strength and wisdom emerge out of this Dragon-Snake combination. This child will have an affinity for helping others, taking proactive action to realize her goals. With the Dragon as her ascendant, she is more outgoing and wants to excel as a leader. She dedicates all energy to her convictions, so she will plan

and organize her actions seriously. The Snake is passionate and the Dragon inner self is idealistic. This is a forceful combination, high-spirited yet tenacious and persevering. This child has a natural affinity for success and power.

THE SNAKE ASCENDANT—TIME OF BIRTH IS BETWEEN 9 A.M. AND 10:59 A.M.
The pure Snake is like no other vault in the zodiac; no amount of prying will loosen these lips. Even those who are closest to this child might be left guessing when it comes to her dreams and aspirations. But her silence does not mean a plan is not already in full swing. Once this Snake sets her eye upon a goal, she tenaciously fights for it. However, this special child may prefer to wait for things to come her way. Patient and intelligent, she has enduring and deep convictions and is very intuitive. Others look to her to identify what is important. This enigmatic child will be a trendsetter in her own right.

THE HORSE ASCENDANT—TIME OF BIRTH IS BETWEEN 11 A.M. AND 12:59 P.M.
The Horse ascendant encourages this child to go play outside and take part in activity with others. This Snake will have a sunnier disposition, which promotes a more liberal, fast-paced lifestyle than most Snakes have. Others born under this sign may hold on viciously to their possessions, but not those aligned with the Horse ascendant. She may be quite popular with the opposite sex, since the Horse and the Snake attract a lot of attention. With the Horse as her inner self, this Snake child is outspoken and energetic. Unlike the stable Snake sign, the Horse will influence this child to be very flexible, and she will not hesitate to change her mind quickly if the wind suddenly blows from a different direction.

THE SHEEP ASCENDANT—TIME OF BIRTH IS BETWEEN 1 P.M. AND 2:59 P.M.
The Snake is a cautious and factual personality, not given to speculation or emotional outburst, while the Sheep is the big spender ruled by the heart. Hopefully, the two may counteract each other and produce a child who knows how to budget both time and money. The Sheep as the inner self would love to

take part in many philanthropic causes and cares for others with great compassion. This child may grow to be quite the artist or musician with the Snake's deep thought and wisdom and the creative voice of the Sheep ascendant.

THE MONKEY ASCENDANT—TIME OF BIRTH IS BETWEEN 3 P.M. AND 4:59 P.M.

A born competitor and worthy adversary for the most cunning of opponents, the Snake and Monkey combination lends razor-sharp wits to the Snake's unmatched talents of persuasion and perseverance. This ambitious yet enchanting child will find great ease in many endeavors she embarks upon. The Monkey ascendant is clever and calculating, while the Snake personality never gives up or gives in. Here is a winning combination, which matches good strategy with vision and creativity. The Monkey ascendant will teach the Snake to network with finesse and get the best deal without stepping on anyone's toes.

THE ROOSTER ASCENDANT—TIME OF BIRTH IS BETWEEN 5 P.M. AND 6:59 P.M.

Arriving in the Rooster hour, this efficient and astute child could be destined for great things. The Rooster ascendant always wants to get the job done, fiercely out to achieve goals and show others her capabilities. She needs little or no motivation. A strong communicator, this is one Snake that will not be hard to figure out. Messages from Roosters are rarely fuzzy. A lover of details, she is sure to demand and receive the best. This intellectual Snake child will have a flamboyant and colorful side with the Rooster as her inner self. The critical Rooster also makes this Snake child more outspoken and aggressive.

THE DOG ASCENDANT—TIME OF BIRTH IS BETWEEN 7 P.M. AND 8:59 P.M.

This loveable child possesses the warmth of her Dog ascendant and her friendly and trusting attributes will make for a more affectionate Snake. People are naturally attracted to the Dog, who makes friends rather effortlessly. This amiable Snake will be less high-strung than others, choosing to be more levelheaded and practical. The loyalty of this child will be impenetrable, and she will endure any cost to right any wrong against those she loves. With the Dog as her inner self, this Snake child will be cooperative and less selfish. The Dog is not jealous or demanding by nature and knows how to get along with others; this helps her Snake half to think less of herself and more of her team.

THE BOAR ASCENDANT—TIME OF BIRTH IS BETWEEN 9 P.M. AND 10:59 P.M.
Generosity runs thick through the rich blood of the Boar sign. With this ascendant, this entertaining child will be the ideal hostess, with the Snake's charm and the lavish ways of the sensual Boar. Friends will flock to parties and gatherings, knowing that they will always be well taken care of in her presence. With the Boar as her inner self, this Snake child will not have large privacy issues, because the Boar is very open and giving—sometimes to a fault. However, the Snake is wise and calculating while the Boar side tends to be trusting and naive. A middle-of-the-road approach will produce a child who communicates well and has great presence and stamina. Here is wisdom and kindheartedness combined.

93

Famous Persons Born in the Year of the Snake

Pablo Picasso

Yasser Arafat

Greta Garbo

Henri Matisse

Mahatma Gandhi

Abraham Lincoln

King Hassan II of Morocco

Princess Grace of Monaco

Mao Tse-Tung

Oprah Winfrey

Mary Pickford

Henry Ford II

John F. Kennedy

Katharine Graham

Tony Blair

Howard Hughes

Seni Pramoj

Audrey Hepburn

Dick Cheney

Edgar Allan Poe

Jacqueline Onassis

Johannes Brahms

J. Paul Getty

Benazir Bhutto

Franz Schubert

Gamal Abdel Nasser

Indira Gandhi

Martha Stewart

As a treat to your child, please read the Snake's story,
"The Legend of Lady White Snake," which follows.

THE SNAKE'S STORY

"THE LEGEND OF LADY WHITE SNAKE"

Thousands of years ago, when the world was young and people and animals were friends and could talk to one another, there lived a poor young farmer in a hut near the edge of a forest. His name was Ming Xiao, but everyone called him Ming for short. Besides his meager income from farming the tiny plot of land behind his hut, Ming had a small raft he built from tree logs, and he would often take the raft out to the deep part of the river near his home to fish. He never caught much to boast of, but he enjoyed fishing both as a way of feeding himself and as a sport.

But although he was poor, so was everyone else around him. Ming was a quiet and helpful young man who was content with his lot in life and got along well with others. Both his parents had passed away, and as an only child, Ming inherited whatever little his parents owned and did not know how to live any way aside from the peasant lifestyle of his mother and father. His life was rather simple and uneventful until one summer day, when there was a forest fire that changed Ming's life forever. At first, it was just a plume of smoke far up in the hills, but as the day progressed, the winds kept blowing the fire toward Ming's village and the river behind it. The frightened animals of the forest all ran toward the river, and those who could swim took refuge there. It was the only place with water to protect them from the flames.

Ming grabbed his few possessions—his cooking pot, some tools, sleeping mat, and bedding—put everything on his raft, and was just about to push off into the river with his long pole when he took pity on a few animals stranded on the river's edge. Although his raft, now filled with his belongings, was not big enough to take many passengers, the young man invited a fox, a deer, and a Snake to share his raft as he made for the safety of the river. The three animals were grateful for his kindness. After the fire burned itself out, Ming brought them all back to shore and they thanked him again for saving them.

The young man was able to rebuild his hut quickly, but he became even more dependent on his fishing skills since the fire had destroyed the small crop he had planted. Ming was pleasantly surprised and very happy when the fox and the deer returned to help him rebuild. The fox was the more talkative of the two and would always order the good-natured deer around. The deer did not mind hauling firewood, clearing debris, or even allowing Ming to ride on his back. One evening, when the fox had left, the deer stayed late to tell Ming a secret.

"In an old cave deep in the hills, I know of a treasure buried under a big rock shaped like a turtle," said the deer. "Since I have no need for gold and silver, I would like you to have it as a reward for your kindness in saving me from the fire. However, we can only go there during the night, so you must bring an oil lamp and I will lead the way."

Ming followed the deer to the hidden treasure and was amazed at the riches that were buried there. The deer then helped the young man carry the buried treasure home, and they buried it under the newly constructed hut. The next day, the fox arrived and found out about the treasure. He was very happy for Ming, whom he considered a dear friend, but as usual, the fox had many bright ideas and advice that he couldn't wait to give.

"You must build a bigger, better place to protect the treasure. Let's spend some money putting a fence around your property, and we must purchase better materials like bricks and stones. Let's get a boat instead of that old raft to go fishing," suggested the fox, without even stopping to catch his breath.

Although Ming and the deer resisted many of the fox's grand suggestions, they did make improvements to Ming's home, built a fence around it, and purchased a beautiful boat. Eventually, everyone began to notice that Ming had come into a great deal of money. Added to this growing suspicion and curiosity, the fox got bolder and boasted to some jealous neighbors that Ming had found a treasure. One of the neighbors was a scheming man who was related to the town sheriff. He claimed to know of a merchant in town who was robbed and had lost a large sum of gold and silver. This merchant said he was robbed late at night around the same time that Ming claimed to have found the cache of precious metals.

Without even a trial, Ming was promptly arrested and thrown into jail by the sheriff. The rich merchant, the sheriff, and the jealous neighbor then took all Ming's possessions as their own. The fox tried to visit Ming in jail, but he was chased away, and the shy deer dared not come near the town's jail, as he was afraid of being killed. The poor young man was despondent and resigned to spending a long, harsh winter in prison.

"Ay, yah," he lamented, "how could my good fortune turn into such misfortune?"

"Now, even my friends, the fox and the deer, are too scared to visit or help me. I shall probably die alone in jail."

Then, at the feast of the Excited Insects, just before the onset of the Vernal Equinox, Snakes awoke from their hibernation and started to bite people who ventured out into the fields and the hillside. This was a yearly occurrence and Snakes were greatly feared in the village. Many who were bitten often did not survive, especially if the very poisonous green bamboo Snake bit them. One night, as Ming was sleeping on the floor of his cell, a large white Snake crawled into the tiny hovel and bit him on the foot.

"Ouch," cried Ming as he woke up instantly. His eyes widened in pain and terror as he saw the Snake and felt the intense pain in his foot.

"Oh, no, I've been bitten by a Snake!"

Upon looking closely at the Snake, Ming recognized it as the one he had saved a year ago from the fire.

"Such ingratitude! How could you be so cruel? Is this how you repay me for my kindness?" the young man asked the snake.

As Ming clutched his foot in agony, the Snake turned into a beautiful lady in white who was holding a bottle of little round pills. She smiled at the young man as she gave him the bottle and said:

"I am the Snake you saved from the fire. I have come to help you in your hour of need. Here, take three of these little pills and you will be cured of my bite."

Ming could not believe that there was such a lovely lady in front of him, much less the fact that she was offering him an antidote for the snakebite. She wore the rich, flowing silk robes of a lady of the emperor's court and looked out of place in such an awful place like a jail.

"This will counteract the venom," she said softly, "as like cures like."

Ming swallowed the three round pills and immediately felt better as the pain left his foot and the wound dried up. The lady turned into a white Snake again and left as silently as she came. Ming shook his head and pinched his cheek to see if it was all a bad dream, but the bottle of little round pills still in his hands told him it was all true.

The next evening, Lady White Snake returned and told Ming that the chief guard at the prison had been bitten by another Snake, and that Ming should take three pills from the bottle she gave him and help that victim. Ming banged loudly on the jail door until they would listen to him. When he told them he could help the chief guard who was just bitten on the leg, all the guards were surprised at Ming's knowledge of such news and finally took him to see their chief. After swallowing the antidote, the chief guard got well and was very happy to be cured so quickly and completely. However, he could not release Ming from jail because Ming was still considered a thief and had to serve his sentence.

On the third evening, Lady White Snake returned again and told Ming that the magistrate's wife had been bitten by yet another Snake that she had stepped on as she journeyed into the next town to visit her sister. This time, the chief of the guards lost no time in bringing Ming to the magistrate's house and vouching that Ming had cured him the day before. After the young man gave the magistrate's wife the antidote and she was cured, the magistrate heard more about Ming's arrest without a hearing or a trial and had the case investigated. This time, the rich merchant, the jealous neighbor, and the sheriff were arrested and questioned. They finally confessed that they made the whole story up, based on what the jealous neighbor had told them. All the three evildoers were now thrown in jail, and Ming was released and his gold and silver were returned to him.

However, the timely appearance of Lady White Snake in his life and how she saved Ming from a terrible injustice had a profound influence on the young

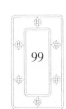

man. He remembered his year of great fortune and what was the unfortunate outcome of wealth or a lavish lifestyle. Ming decided to give away all his riches to the poor and to become a monk. Ming shaved his head, donned saffron robes, and dedicated his life to serving the people who came to the temple. When Lady White Snake saw how sincere Ming was, she appeared once more and gave him the formula for how to make the little round pills that were the antidote to any snakebite. People from all around the province would come to the temple to get the pills, and Ming would help them without asking for any payment. Ming never saw the deer, the fox, or the beautiful Lady White Snake again, but he knew in his heart that if he ever needed help, his true friends would find a way of helping him.

CHAPTER SEVEN

THE HORSE

The Seventh Lunar Sign

The Horse personality is

Keen perception combined with speed and progress.

An independent spirit, here is a

Happy child spirit gifted with superior

Instincts rich in self-reliance.

Practical yet brave and

Spontaneous, the Horse likes to

Be involved in challenging activity.

A sharp, mercurial mind and restless

Spirit make him the

Unparalleled adventurer of

The lunar cycle.

His motto is: **SUCCESS IS WHAT WE MAKE FOR OURSELVES!**

THE HORSE'S BRANCH

CHINESE NAME FOR THE HORSE: *Ma*

RANK: Seventh

HOURS OF THE HORSE: From 11 A.M. to 12:59 P.M.*

DIRECTION OF THIS BRANCH: Directly south

SEASON AND PRINCIPAL MONTH: Summer and June

CORRESPONDS TO THE WESTERN SIGN: Gemini, the Twins

FIXED ELEMENT: Fire

STEM: Yang, or masculine

*Ascendant: *Children who are born during the two-hour segment of the day ruled by the Horse sign will have this sign as their ascendant and will display affinity for people born under this particular sign, as well as have many of the distinct character traits that identify the Horse sign.*

FIVE CYCLES* OF THE LUNAR YEARS OF THE HORSE
IN THE WESTERN CALENDAR

START DATE		END DATE	ELEMENT OF THE YEAR
January 21, 1966	to	February 8, 1967	Fire
February 7, 1978	to	January 27, 1979	Earth
January 27, 1990	to	February 14, 1991	Metal
February 12, 2002	to	January 31, 2003	Water
January 31, 2014	to	February 18, 2015	Wood

* A cycle on the lunar horoscope equals twelve years. Five cycles completes sixty years.

Note: One who is born on the day before the start of the lunar year of the Horse, e.g. January 26, 1990, will belong to the animal sign before the Horse, which is the Snake, the sixth lunar sign. One who is born on the day after the end of the lunar year of the Horse, e.g., February 15, 1991, belongs to the animal sign following the Horse, which is the Sheep, the eighth lunar sign.

THE HORSE SIGN

SUCCESS IS WHAT WE MAKE FOR OURSELVES

The Horse Personality

The personality of the seventh earth branch is named *Wu*. This is symbolized by the Horse's sign. The *Wu* is an adventurer who seeks excitement and activity. A child born under this seventh earth branch loves to be in tune with his environment. He walks early, probably talks early, is coordinated in movements, and develops an early appreciation for sports or games of skill.

The Horse character is a rugged individualist who is popular and known for his sharp mind and quick reactions. Many horse children are left-handed and are twins. Since this lunar sign corresponds to the Western sign Gemini, the natives of the Horse sign tend to be quick-witted and mercurial. The Horse child is fiercely independent and loves to do things for himself. He hates to wait for others or be told to hold on and takes things one at a time. He loves the outdoors and needs plenty of exercise and open space to vent his seemingly inexhaustible energy. Although he is not the whining, complaining child that clings to his parents, he can be self-centered and stubborn. He needs to find new things to occupy his time, or he will easily get distracted and restless.

Not one to follow fixed schedules or be tied down by too much routine, the Horse favors diversity and change. He could be a happy-go-lucky personality who loves to do things at the spur of the moment. Not one to hesitate or spend a lot of time thinking things over, the Horse acts impulsively. He is easily stimulated and loves to be part of any action going on around him. Attracted to new inventions and anything unconventional, the Horse child can be inconsistent and irresponsible unless he is led by firm hands and taught the benefits of discipline and organization. The Horse child is likely to be ingenious and resourceful, but not likely to persevere as other signs.

Sociable and adaptable, this child is noted for forming relationships early and being able to guess what is on other people's minds. Just a hint and he will catch on and finish the sentence for you. Because he loves his independence and possesses an adventurous spirit, he can also be rebellious and hardheaded. His many-faceted personality is very colorful and he needs a good deal of variety in life. This child is most happy when he is multitasking. It does not spoil his concentration. He will be able to keep in step with several things and his performance is actually better when he does many tasks at the same time. He learns quickly and is able to improvise and work around problems on his own. The competitive Horse child will try to top his own performance and break records just for the heck of it. Fun-loving, happy, and cooperative by nature, the Horse is competent and perceptive and his agile mental and physical abilities will constantly put him in the forefront of action.

Birth Order and Sibling Rivalry

*FIRSTBORN OR ONLY CHILD

The Horse as the firstborn or only child is fiercely independent and self-reliant. He is confident and in charge of his environment and will not allow others, especially the younger ones, to wrestle control from him in any way. He is easily agitated when held back or criticized and can be headstrong and opinionated. At times, he is indifferent to younger siblings when they do not take his advice or follow his leadership quickly. Impatient and restless, he does not make a good teacher and would rather take off on his own and do his own thing if he does not find the prompt action or appreciation from the younger ones. He will not lack friends or admirers, as he can be very charming and delightful. This Horse, however, is most likely to be in step with his parents' pace and could march to their tune without missing a beat.

MIDDLE OR LATER-BORN CHILD

Here is a restless adventurer who tends to be impatient and competitive. If he is a twin, it will be hard to keep up or keep hold of him. The Horse child as the middle or later-born tends to be more self-centered than the firstborn. An elitist, he is

* When a child is born five years after another child, he or she is also considered a firstborn child.

proud to hold his own and will rarely accept help or advice from anyone aside from his parents. No doubt he will be talented and will show his skills early in life. However, he tends to dissipate his energies if he cannot get instant gratification, and he tends to lose interest or get bored easily. Because success comes easily to the Horse personality, he often does not value what he has. He becomes more realistic only after he has had a few hard-fought battles under his belt. He can be kind to his siblings, so long as they do not encroach on his space or push him around.

YOUNGEST OR LAST-BORN CHILD

This is a happy position for a Horse child to be born in, as he marches to his own drummer and is content to be in his own busy, busy world. He is not easily upset by changes in his schedules, delays and complications do not distress him, and he can change and adapt quickly with a smile. He is fascinated by action, excitement, and sports. Expressive and outgoing, this child is honest and straightforward and does not hide or bottle up feelings. He could have a big outburst one moment and then forget about it in an instant. He is not likely to sulk or carry grudges and gets along well with his older siblings, provided they do not baby or smother him too much. Above all, he wants his freedom to do his own thing and express himself.

Ascendants

In Chinese horoscopes, the two-hour segment ruling the time of birth is known as the ascendant sign. This can also be referred to as the child's "inner self."

The time of birth used to determine the ascendant is always the local time in the place of birth.

For a child born in the Year of the Horse:

THE RAT ASCENDANT—TIME OF BIRTH IS BETWEEN 11 P.M. AND 12:59 A.M.

This child will be one who chooses places of work and education to be close to his home. The Rat ascendant helps strengthen bonds to the family and other loved ones. No matter where his commitments may lead, this sentimental Horse's heart will always be at home. This combination also fosters an active imagination and excellent money-managing skills. With his Rat ascendant, this child is diligent and skillful with his words. Energetic and efficient, this Horse child will be able to look before he leaps with the crafty Rat as his inner self.

THE OX ASCENDANT—TIME OF BIRTH IS BETWEEN 1 A.M. AND 2:59 A.M.

The stalwart Ox ascendant makes for a Horse that you can depend on. Many Horses follow their hearts first and their minds second, but the stable Ox ascendant helps reverse this innocent thinking. Nevertheless, he will still be adventurous and extremely social. This child will be very popular with others, especially those of the opposite sex. Sportive yet more consistent and persevering, the child with the Ox as his inner self is more reserved and careful in what he says and does. He works at a slow pace but is surer of himself and checks his information before committing himself fully.

THE TIGER ASCENDANT—TIME OF BIRTH IS BETWEEN 3 A.M. AND 4:59 A.M.

With the Tiger's confidence and passion, many of this Horse's dreams and aspirations may very well be possible and dramatic to boot. The Horse's intuition is almost always on target, while the fearless Tiger encourages him to follow his impulses. Together, this combination may create a child who is adventurous, independent, and spontaneous. This free spirit optimistically races through life, finding friends and alliances wherever he goes. The captivating Tiger ascendant gives depth and idealism to the strong-willed Horse, who always wants to go his own way and hates to have his liberty curtailed. This is a child with warmth, intelligence, and passion who is as responsive and outgoing as a little whirlwind.

THE RABBIT ASCENDANT—TIME OF BIRTH IS BETWEEN 5 A.M. AND 6:59 A.M.

While not as outgoing as other Horses, this child with a Rabbit ascendant will possess the same natural charisma of the Horse sign, but in a slightly more reserved and cautious form. He thinks before he speaks and has excellent control over emotions, especially in matters of the heart. In regard to finances as well as adventure, he will know when to sacrifice and when to spend, unlike many of his Horse peers. With the suave Rabbit as his inner self, this Horse child is diplomatic and astute in manner. He will not be as impatient as other horses and knows how to manipulate others skillfully without ever provoking their anger.

THE DRAGON ASCENDANT—TIME OF BIRTH IS BETWEEN 7 A.M. AND 8:59 A.M.
This powerful Horse child chooses to learn by experience, not guidance, thank you very much. The dynamic Dragon ascendant intensifies the Horse's freewheeling manner, encouraging more daring adventures, even for a Horse child. With the mighty Dragon ascendant, this Horse child feels quite omnipotent at times and will love to run to the edge of the precipice to prove a point and drive his parents crazy. With the Dragon as his inner self, this child is rich in self-confidence but also realizes his responsibilities and duties, and he will be more conventional in his love and respect for those in authority. He has good self-esteem and will provide leadership if he can learn to be more tolerant and patient. On the whole, he is self-reliant.

THE SNAKE ASCENDANT—TIME OF BIRTH IS BETWEEN 9 A.M. AND 10:59 A.M.
With the Snake as his second self, possibly a quieter, more introspective child emerges from the combination of Horse and Snake. With the wise strategy of "measure twice, cut once," success may find him faster than it will other Horses in the long run. The mystical Snake is an intelligent sign who knows the power of confidentiality and restraint, which really aids the Horse, especially in his wild youth. This Horse child is more deliberate and coolheaded in making decisions, as the Snake inner self can be controlling and more possessive than the carefree horse—a thinker and a doer combination that can be very astute in business.

THE HORSE ASCENDANT—TIME OF BIRTH IS BETWEEN 11 A.M. AND 12:59 P.M.
With its own sign as the ascendant, this double horsepower means twice the adventure in half the time, maybe more. The Horse's strengths and weaknesses

are magnified with his twin as his ascendant. He will be active in sports and activities and be a master at social interaction. As he is prone to juggling many commitments, don't be surprised if he shows some fickleness when making a promise or maybe even forgetting that he made the promise. This is a competitive and workaholic combination who needs constant stimulation and activity. At his best, he can be practical, superefficient, and carefree. At his worst, he is selfish and irresponsible. He may be very good at sports or anything that requires lightning-fast reflexes or quick thinking—an air traffic controller?

THE SHEEP ASCENDANT—TIME OF BIRTH IS BETWEEN 1 P.M. AND 2:59 P.M.

With the kindly Sheep as his ascendant, this Horse child is a lover of the arts and his fellow man. This creative and demonstrative child will expect as much as he gives. This Horse is one that follows through and will be disappointed when others do not do the same. Oftentimes thin-skinned, he may need constant encouragement and self-esteem mending. With the Sheep as his inner self, this Horse child looks to his parents, siblings, and teachers for support and will need mentoring and guidance. This Horse will still know how to party, and with such a loving and generous personality, he could be very much the social butterfly.

THE MONKEY ASCENDANT—TIME OF BIRTH IS BETWEEN 3 P.M. AND 4:59 P.M.

Some Horses run to explore and have fun, but with the clever Monkey riding this Horse, this one will surely run to win. Beware of the moments when this child doesn't win, because Monkeys do not take disappointment well at all. This combination produces agility of both mind and body. Also, the charm and effortless social skills of his ascendant could make this Horse very persuasive and inventive. Both signs in this combination are flexible and practical and do not like to dwell on unimportant issues. They both are problem solvers and more concerned with finding solutions instead of blame. He is a smart and productive personality who really knows how to strike out for himself.

THE ROOSTER ASCENDANT—TIME OF BIRTH IS BETWEEN 5 P.M. AND 6:59 P.M.

With this ascendant, this Horse child is a lover of order and details; the eccentric Rooster is the ultimate critic and perfectionist. Others may pull their hair out at such a meticulous agenda, but love it or hate it, he is not going to change. Observant peers will notice that this diligent Horse delivers over and beyond expectations. He is definitely one you can count on. He rarely dwells upon the past, and his confident outlook supplies the energy to meet his own high ambitions and standards. Both signs in this combination have colorful and often flamboyant traits, so this brilliant child could display genius while being self-centered and opinionated.

THE DOG ASCENDANT—TIME OF BIRTH IS BETWEEN 7 P.M. AND 8:59 P.M.

Strong, with a strict code of ethics, the Horse child with a Dog ascendant is a lover of justice and fair play. This child's mind will be sharp and objective, just like any good detective and champion of the less fortunate. With the reasonable Dog as his inner self, this special child will be faithfully devoted to family and friends and protect them at all costs. Not as adventurous as other Horses, a child with this ascendant feels comfortable being conventional and close to home. A good communicator and intelligent mediator, the Dog brings warmth to the quick-witted but often impersonal Horse personality. This child is naturally outspoken, and volunteer activities and social groups will find their most active member to be the Horse with a Dog ascendant.

THE BOAR ASCENDANT—TIME OF BIRTH IS BETWEEN 9 P.M. AND 10:59 P.M.

Throughout life, this child with the Boar ascendant will always play well with others and be liked for his generosity and big heart. He is a team player who will often act as mediator to the rest of the group. The Horse is fast to respond and enjoys sports and adventures, while the Boar inner self does have a hefty appetite for excitement and the finer things in life, too. This sociable combination produces a more cooperative and mellow personality who still enjoys a good challenge, but who is not rebellious or confrontational when met with

resistance. The Boar ascendant heightens the beauty of this engaging Horse, producing an enticing combination who knows how to motivate others as well as help others unselfishly with his special gifts.

Famous Persons Born in the Year of the Horse

Neil Armstrong	Boris Yeltsin
Earl of Snowdon	Lenin
Rembrandt	Leonid Brezhnev
Roberto Rossellini	Otto Preminger
Patty Hearst	King Faisal
Agnes Moorehead	Thomas Edison
Pearl Bailey	Kurt Waldheim
Theodore Roosevelt	Alexander Solzhenitsyn
Chris Evert	Leonard Bernstein
Billy Graham	Anwar Sadat
Nelson Mandela	Franklin D. Roosevelt
Barbra Streisand	Ulysses S. Grant
Paul McCartney	Duke of Windsor

*As a treat to your child, please read the Horse's story,
"A Gift from Heaven," which follows.*

THE HORSE'S STORY

"A GIFT FROM HEAVEN"

Many thousands of years ago, high up in the cold northern mountains of the Middle Kingdom, there lived a tribe who raised Horses and mountain goats for a living. They were hardy and independent people who loved their freedom and special way of life. Among the tribe was a family with four sons and a young daughter of about ten, who tended the goats for the family. She was the youngest child, and while her older brothers took care of the Horses, she tended the goats and smaller animals. The girl's name was Lena, and although she was small and skinny, Lena was energetic and helpful and she enjoyed talking to all the animals she met. She was especially kind to sick animals, whom she nursed back to health with great patience and love.

Life was harsh in the cold northern mountains and everyone was expected to work hard and help out, including the children. Although Lena was the youngest and a girl with four older brothers, she had to milk the goats, take them to the pasture, draw water, help her mother with chores, collect firewood, and spin the yarn they got from their long-haired goats in the wintertime. She had an orange-colored sheepdog named Pipa who followed her everywhere.

One cold winter's day, as Lena was driving the small band of goats through a narrow mountain pass on her way home, she heard the small cry of a young animal in distress. Looking through the bushes, she found a newborn foal whimpering in the cold. Taking off her warm padded jacket, she wrapped the foal in her coat and carried the baby Horse home. It was a strange-looking Horse, with four distinct colors: white, black, red, and yellow, in a coat with marble-like markings. The swirl-like design looked like dark and light clouds mixed together in a wavy pattern, and right on the top of the foal's forehead was the shape of a "fairy herb" mushroom. This particular mushroom was much prized, as it was valued as a cure for all types of illness and was usually

taken to promote long life and good health. Once Lena saw the marking on the foal's forehead, she decided to name her new friend Ling-Tzi, which was Chinese for "the fairy mushroom." At first, everyone made fun of this funny-looking foal and really did not think it was strong enough to survive. However, under the careful and nurturing hands of Lena, Ling-Tzi began to flourish and gain weight. Lena would not let her new charge out of sight, so she took Ling-Tzi out with her when she brought the goats to pasture. Pipa also grew attached to the skinny female foal, whose spindly legs often looked too thin to support her. An unruly tuft of mane sprouted on Ling-Tzi's forehead just above the "fairy mushroom" mark. Having four swirling colors really made Ling-Tzi's coat look like everything was painted on. The she-Horse acquired the nickname of "painted pony" and everyone would even joke that Ling-Tzi was actually the first "Horse-goat," too strange and ugly to really be either Horse or goat. In a way, Lena was grateful for her Horse's ungainly appearance, as her father and brothers did not want the painted she-Horse to join their band of stately stallions. Her weird foundling would have stood out like a sore thumb among the proud and elegant Horses of the tribe.

Lena loved her Horse dearly because she could talk to Ling-Tzi and Ling-Tzi would only talk to her. Not only could these two friends talk freely, but eventually they found that they could communicate by way of thoughts to a point where spoken words were no longer needed. As the Horse grew into her first year, she began to fill out and look much more like other Horses. Of course, by now everyone knew the painted pony by her strange markings, and Lena was never far from her friend's side. When others heard Ling-Tzi neighing, Lena would actually hear what the Horse was telling her. Together, they would make up songs to sing as they tended the goats and also gathered firewood or went about doing chores. Lena, who always longed for a sister, felt that Ling-Tzi was sent as a gift from heaven. The Horse and the girl addressed each other as sister, as they communicated either by voice or thoughts. As Ling-Tzi grew larger and stronger, the Horse would carry Lena and the firewood on her back and did more than her fair share of herding the goats with the help of Pipa.

One day, as they ventured near another farm, Ling-Tzi told Lena that she could hear an argument going on inside a hut that was located quite a distance downhill.

"Oh, my, I am afraid to tell you, sister, that there seems to be a terrible argument in that hut, and there could be some violence to come," whispered Ling-Tzi to the girl.

"What can we do?" asked Lena. "If it's too dangerous, maybe we should leave."

"No," answered Ling-Tzi, "we cannot leave until we know more. Let's just keep out of sight and watch from on top of the hill. Perhaps we may be of some help."

After a while, the shouting and arguing stopped and two men emerged from the hut, got on their Horses quickly, and left. In a short while, a thin column of smoke rose from the hut and Ling-Tzi immediately said to Lena:

"Quick, sister, get on my back, we must go down right away to help the people in the hut before the fire goes out of control."

Lena was taken aback because she was not even aware that the hut was on fire, but she got on the Horse's back and they raced to the hut just in time to help untie an old couple and escape the fire. As it turned out, the two men who were trying to rob the old couple had started the fire when they found out that there wasn't any money or anything of value in the hut. Lena wanted to tell the old man and his wife that Ling-Tzi should get all the credit for saving their lives, but the Horse spoke to Lena through her mind and told her not to say anything.

"Sister, they would not believe us if we told them the truth. It is best not to say anything at this time," flashed the Horse's message silently to Lena.

"I understand, dear sister," flashed Lena back in return.

This teamwork of helping others, without expecting anything in return, went on for several years. True to her name, Ling-Tzi taught Lena how to identify herbs, spices, roots, and berries. Together they made up healing potions to help her large family and other people of her tribe, including, of course, sick animals. They often found the fairy herb, which Ling-Tzi was named after, high in the cold areas and they would dry the herb and slice it paper-thin to use as medicine.

When Lena reached the age of fifteen, she was betrothed in marriage, as was the custom of her time. The marriage was arranged not only by her parents but also with the approval of the tribal elders who were always concerned about new members joining their tribe or members leaving to join another tribe. In this case, everyone was pleased because the prospective groom lived in an enclave close by and was believed to have much property and livestock. He was known to be wealthy, but no one knew of his exact age or profession. He had been married once before, but his wife had died and left no children.

Lena had little dowry but begged her parents to allow her to bring Ling-Tzi with her to her new home. They agreed, as they knew the two were inseparable. The groom to be did not have many demands except that his new wife be young and healthy, so as to bear him children. Everyone was for the arranged marriage except Lena's Horse, who kept a low profile and did not express any opinion, even to Lena.

"Why are you so quiet, dear sister?" Lena asked. "Are you angry with me?"

"I have a deep foreboding for you," said Ling-Tzi. "Yet, I do not know what it is, for I have never felt this strange kind of fear before."

Lena pleaded with Ling Tzi. "Please do not be concerned, sister. My parents have agreed that I can bring you with me to my new home and you know I will never leave you."

As was the custom with arranged marriages, the bride and groom did not see each other until after the wedding. The marriage was conducted through matchmakers and go-betweens who worked out all the details with both parties. Lena's wedding was in the spring, when the first flowers started to emerge from the frost. It was a happy time and everyone attended. Lena's big brothers and their wives all came, and Lena's parents and aunts, uncles, and cousins also had a big reunion to celebrate her wedding. Because she was always a bit shy and very quiet, her family thought her to be rather homely and difficult to marry off. When they had the offer of marriage from a man of wealth and property, they all jumped at it without further thought or much investigation. Everyone knew little of the groom and even the matchmakers were sketchy on information about him, but they made up lovely stories of his wealth, his intelligence, and his importance to impress the entire tribe.

While the bride had her face covered by an intricate headdress and veil, the groom arrived in rich red and saffron robes without covering his face. While he did look like a rich baron in his expensive clothing, the groom was portly and balding and sported a rather wild mustache and black beard. He did not seem friendly and did not speak much, but everyone took this aloofness as a sign of his higher station in life and deferred to him graciously. No relative or friends showed up from the groom's side. The groom's servants worked efficiently and did not speak to anyone. They seemed in a hurry to return home and rode in their own wagon. Immediately after the wedding feast, Lena and her new husband left in his carriage loaded with their wedding gifts of blankets, clothing, pots and pans, and even furniture given by her family. Ling-Tzi followed the servants' wagon with the rest of the bride's belongings and Pipa followed the Horse like a restless shadow. The bride and groom rode for an hour without any conversation, the carriage turning and twisting through the mountain passes until night fell quietly as they entered a gorge covered by a canopy of huge trees.

Before the carriage even came to a complete stop, the groom's servants had already stood outside the door to usher the new bride into her home. The house was big and cold and dark. Its musty odor spoke of a long period of not being aired or even occupied. Lanterns and candles were lit, but no amount of light could cheer up the cold and dark house Lena had entered.

"Sister, can you hear me?" flashed the bride's thought silently to her Horse. "I'm frightened of this place!"

"I'm here, just outside your window, Lena," came the Horse's mental reply.

Her new husband roughly yanked Lena's arm to show her in to a large chamber and he pushed her through the doorway. Lena felt disoriented in the large room, but she composed herself and took off her veil to look at her new husband. She was surprised to see him face to face for the first time, and he did not speak but glared at Lena with fierce red eyes. It only took a second for Lena to transmit the image of the groom to the mind of Ling-Tzi.

"You must flee, my dear sister!" screamed the horse outside the window. "You have married a monster pretending to be a man. Jump out the window onto my back, and we will leave this horrid place at once."

Lena looked up at her husband just in time to see him take out a dagger and grab her braided hair. As she pushed him away, he was able to cut off her braid, but Lena managed to leap out the window onto Ling-Tzi's back. Pipa barked in alarm as the groom jumped down the window right after Lena. But Ling-Tzi was ready for him. She reared her hind legs and kicked the groom with all her might right in his belly. He fell like a sack of grain to the ground and did not get up.

"Hold on tight, sister. Do not look back," said the Horse to Lena.

The threesome rode through the night back to their tribe. The next day Lena told everyone about her monster husband and how he tried to kill her. They saw her long braid missing and her clothing torn. The men in her family got on their Horses and rode to the gorge with Lena and Ling-Tzi leading the way. They found the dark house, but it was empty. Neither the groom nor any of his servants were around. All Lena's belongings were still loaded on the wagon, so they knew they were in the right place.

"This must be a demon's lair by the evil odor that fills this place," concluded the angry relatives of the bride. "Let us take back our bride's property and leave quickly before the monster returns."

However, Ling-Tzi led them to some footprints that looked like bear tracks, and at the end of the trail was the dead body of a huge black bear with hoof marks on its stomach.

Everyone understood without any words being spoken that this was the monster masquerading as the groom, and they were very grateful that Ling-Tzi had saved her mistress from being killed or eaten. Meanwhile, Ling-Tzi continued down the path formed by the canopy of trees to investigate a mysterious sound from inside a small wooden shed. The horse started tapping at the shed door and a soft tapping came from the other side of the door. Lena sensed what Ling-Tzi had discovered and approached the small shed with two of her brothers. They quickly broke down the door when they heard muffled cries coming from inside.

Upon opening the shed, they found the real bridegroom, bound and gagged and his clothes ripped from the bear's claws. After they untied him and gave him some water and tended to his injuries, the bridegroom was able to tell his story of being imprisoned by the beast who stole his identity and home. He was immensely grateful to Lena and her Horse for destroying the evil imposter and setting him free.

Lena returned to her village with the true bridegroom. The town rejoiced at Lena's safe return and celebrated the new couple with a large and colorful wedding. Lena and her new husband lived happily in a new home closer to her village, as they did not want to return to the enclave where the beast kept her husband prisoner. They felt so much more a part of the tribe by living close by.

No one ever knew that Lena and her Horse could talk to each other and communicate through their thoughts. Perhaps Pipa did, but the dog wasn't talking, either. Lena, her husband, Ling-Tzi, and Pipa all grew old together, still helping anyone and everyone who needed their help and asking for nothing in return.

CHAPTER EIGHT

THE SHEEP

The Eighth Lunar Sign

The Sheep is nature's artistic child.

Trusting and worthy of trust,

All things are made beautiful in

The gentleness of her care.

The Sheep child is looked upon as

One favored by Fortune

Because of her generous heart.

Charitable and understanding,

She flourishes in quiet harmony—

Always ready to lend a helping hand.

A compassionate and

Kind advocate who excels as

The Peacemaker of the cycle.

Her motto is: **ONE WHO IS TACTFUL POSSESSES
A KIND HEART!**

THE SHEEP'S BRANCH

CHINESE NAME FOR THE SHEEP: *Yáng*

RANK: Eighth

HOURS OF THE SHEEP: From 1 P.M. to 2:59 P.M.*

DIRECTION OF THIS BRANCH: South-southwest

SEASON AND PRINCIPAL MONTH: Summer and July

CORRESPONDS TO THE WESTERN SIGN: Cancer, the Crab

FIXED ELEMENT: Fire

STEM: Yin, or feminine

*Ascendant: *Children who are born during the two-hour segment of the day ruled by the Sheep sign will have this sign as their ascendant and will display affinity for people born under this particular sign, as well as have many of the distinct character traits that identify the Sheep sign.*

FIVE CYCLES* OF THE LUNAR YEARS OF THE SHEEP IN THE WESTERN CALENDAR

START DATE		END DATE	ELEMENT OF THE YEAR
February 9, 1967	to	January 29, 1968	Fire
January 28, 1979	to	February 15, 1980	Earth
February 15, 1991	to	February 3, 1992	Metal
February 1, 2003	to	January 21, 2004	Water
February 19, 2015	to	February 7, 2016	Wood

* A cycle on the lunar horoscope equals twelve years. Five cycles completes sixty years.

Note: One who is born on the day before the start of the lunar year of the Sheep, e.g., February 14, 1991, will belong to the animal sign before the Sheep, which is the Horse sign, the seventh lunar sign. One who is born on the day after the end of the lunar year of the Sheep, e.g., February 4, 1992, belongs to the animal sign following the Sheep, which is the Monkey, the ninth lunar sign.

機智心善 羊

克昌題 美秀畫

THE SHEEP SIGN
ONE WHO IS TACTFUL POSSESSES A KIND HEART

The Sheep Personality

The eighth earth branch of the Chinese lunar cycle is named *Wei* and is symbolized by the Sheep. This is the sign of the good samaritan who is compassionate and caring and loves to be involved in everything that goes on around her. The *Wei* personality wants her world to be sheltered and tranquil. The Chinese believe Sheep children are most likely to be favored with the three blessings: a good home, a good family, and a prosperous life. The Sheep is always well provided for, as the *Wei* character seems most likely to inherit because of her generous ways and sweet nature. Some way, somehow, money, recognition, friends, and the good things in life seem to find their way to the magnetic Sheep personality.

Depending on how she is raised and her family background, the Sheep child tends to be sensitive to her elders and her environment and quite security conscious. Yet the Sheep is also opportunistic by nature and instinctively knows how to fend for herself and, yes, how to use people and circumstances to her own advantage. In spite of her accommodating, polite demeanor, this child could be quick to tears, complaints, and crying foul when she feels neglected, left out, ignored, or offended in the slightest way. However, it is difficult to be angry with the affectionate Sheep for long because she usually forgives and forgets quickly. The Sheep child bonds deeply with her parents, especially her mother, and in her adoring eyes and mind, her parents always know best.

A good listener and generous friend, the patient Sheep always has time for those she loves. Yet she hesitates to question others or disagree openly, and she hates confrontation. This is not to say she does not and cannot use her stronger allies to do the dirty work for her. She is just as effective behind the scenes as more aggressive signs are directing the traffic. The Sheep also expects others to listen to her woes and make allowance for all her shortcomings, among which being late is right at the top of the list. She can also be too sensitive to criticism and loves to ask for advice, which she may or may not take. The emotional Sheep does not have the coping skills of, say, the Rabbit or the thick skin of the

Boar. She is certainly not as dynamic as the Tiger or the Dragon (unless these signs are her ascendant). Yet with that sorrowful look and that tear in her eye, her parents will be amazed at how much she can get away with. On the other hand, the well-mannered Sheep may give the appearance of weakness or timidity, but she is strong and resilient underneath all that soft wool (which she often pulls over our eyes).

The Sheep child is forgiving and charitable beyond reproach. She is touched by sad or hard-luck stories and will volunteer her time and donate her pocket money to help others. She will share whatever she has with her friends without being asked. Blessed with charm and great powers of persuasion, she can melt the hardest of hearts and manages to achieve her goals while being recognized by everyone as the good one.

The Sheep child can be traditional in her outlook and enjoys her creature comforts to the point of selfishness. But she is cultured and elegant and looks for the good in others. The Sheep is not the best judge of character because she is always willing to give others the benefit of the doubt, and she finds it hard to be objective because her emotions tend to color her opinions. She is also easily intimidated or influenced by those in authority. She fears disapproval and abandonment and worries and frets even when there is no reason for it.

But on the whole, she is a good communicator and loves to mother others, and she has a knack for comforting others with her sincere, heartfelt sympathy. She is also good at suggesting ways out of difficulty or negotiating to resolve a touchy problem. As a child, this personality compensates for all her shortcomings with her loving disposition and willingness to help and share. She treasures and nurtures relationships and is a great comfort to her parents and family. The Sheep child gives wholeheartedly of herself and does not demand too much in return. She is capable of teamwork and cooperation.

Birth Order and Sibling Rivalry

*FIRSTBORN OR ONLY CHILD

The Sheep child born in this position enjoys her position in a relaxed and entitled way. She loves to be served and catered to. Nothing is too good for her discerning and expensive taste. She is diligent in her duties and tends to reign over her younger siblings rather than rule. Not a troublemaker, she will try to appease others and opt for settlement if there is a fight or argument.

As a result, the younger ones tend to guilt her out or appeal to her fears and other worries so that she will agree to their wishes and demands. She prefers her environment to be soothing and calm and she works to keep harmony in the family. Too much responsibility stresses her out and makes her melodramatic.

MIDDLE OR LATER-BORN CHILD

The Sheep child who occupies this slot is more likely to be competitive and resilient because she is not under pressure to be the role model. Her performance is excellent in school, as she is organized and not burdened with the responsibility of being number one or the leader. She is not likely to settle for less than perfection and can be hardworking and creative in her own quiet and efficient yet talented way. She will be warm and cooperative with her siblings and is always considerate of their feelings and knows how not to intrude into their space.

YOUNGEST OR LAST-BORN CHILD

This little lamb is happy in this position. Responsibility is a tough word for her and she would rather others carried that burden, leaving her to express her creativity and interests as she pleases. She will be a good student and make friends easily. A social butterfly, she is not one to take life too seriously, for she knows for sure her older siblings and parents are constantly looking out for her wel-

---

* When a child is born five years after another child, he or she is also considered a firstborn child.

fare. Should she fall, there are many arms to catch her. If things are not to her liking, she will certainly complain and bleat incessantly. A bit complacent and selfish at times, this Sheep child can be a skillful negotiator as she works her magic around the contenders and gets them all to cooperate. Like all Sheep, she has a soft spot in her heart for the less fortunate and is always willing to help if she can.

Ascendants

In Chinese horoscopes, the two-hour segment ruling the time of birth is known as the ascendant sign. This can also be referred to as the child's "inner self."

The time of birth used to determine the ascendant is always the local time in the place of birth.

For a child born in the Year of the Sheep:

THE RAT ASCENDANT—TIME OF BIRTH IS BETWEEN 11 P.M. AND 12:59 A.M.
This child will be naturally popular, with the valuable knack of getting and staying on everyone's good side. The Rat ascendant helps support the often overemotional sheep, giving her a backbone and better resilience. The Rat also contributes to this child's communication skills, especially in her role as mediator. She will enjoy the arts and seek out creative outlets to express herself. With the efficient Rat ascendant, this Sheep child is proactive and less likely to worry and complain. The Rat is also more frugal and crafty than the generous Sheep, so this child may actually love to save money and look for bargains. Both signs are devoted to their parents, so this particular child loves to be close to home.

THE OX ASCENDANT—TIME OF BIRTH IS BETWEEN 1 A.M. AND 2:59 A.M.
Unfailingly loyal, she will protect friends and loved ones no matter the sacrifice. It is not surprising that this child is neither fickle nor tardy, like so many other

Sheep children. The nature of the Ox ascendant is order and responsibility. Outside her soft wooly exterior lies a resolute mind and strong willpower. With this ascendant, this Sheep child is not overly sensitive or emotional. She will hide her feelings well under her Ox inner self and be calm and collected under pressure. However, she has the Ox's strong temper and unbending sense of purpose and can be difficult to cross. Don't ever break a promise to her. There will be hell to pay.

THE TIGER ASCENDANT—TIME OF BIRTH IS BETWEEN 3 A.M. AND 4:59 A.M.

The Tiger is never one to indulge in self-pity, no matter how young, old, or down and out. This is unless she has her own television drama or daytime soap opera where she will win an Emmy. This ascendant tells the wallflower Sheep to get out there and make some waves. No surprise, she may fall in love with the splendor of the stage, which will showcase the Tiger's natural flair. The quiet Sheep will balance out the Tiger's spontaneous actions with deep thought and heartfelt generosity. The dramatic Tiger is colorful as the Sheep's inner self and will make this child very artistic and outgoing. There is never a dull moment with her around. She also does not have a clue on how to manage her expenses, so someone has to be in control of the budget.

THE RABBIT ASCENDANT—TIME OF BIRTH IS BETWEEN 5 A.M. AND 6:59 A.M.

This child will not be one to make rash judgments of others because of the Rabbit's objectivity and civil tongue. But while she excels at research, she often lacks the ability to commit. With her Rabbit ascendant, she will prefer living life in the third person, which makes for the ideal negotiator or arbitrator. This child's ability to break down first impressions into quality judgments is right on the mark as well. While the Rabbit's other self does not enjoy being inconvenienced or put out, this does not mean that there will be any lack of generous moments or sympathy from the Sheep personality. Here is a wonderful, tactful, and kind friend who can also be a good confidant and wise adviser.

THE DRAGON ASCENDANT—TIME OF BIRTH IS BETWEEN 7 A.M. AND 8:59 A.M.

The Sheep's imagination and creativity merged with the strength and skill of the Dragon make for quite the powerhouse indeed. The mighty Dragon helps the Sheep listen to criticism and make it work in her favor. This child will hold strongly onto her beliefs and opinions, often influencing her peers with such pure convictions. Enjoying light and breezy times, this child makes time to find an escape with friends and indulge herself with the whims and fancies her Sheep nature dictates. She won't hang on to money long, but you will find her spending it on her friends and on herself with gusto. The Dragon gives her a strong presence.

THE SNAKE ASCENDANT—TIME OF BIRTH IS BETWEEN 9 A.M. AND 10:59 A.M.

Determined and organized, the Snake ascendant helps this Sheep craft her plans and carry them out with great skill. Whatever she decides is her passion, this child will forge ahead and probably revolutionize the field she chooses. This particular Sheep child may keep career goals and dreams quiet, since her inner self finds comfort in discretion. Nothing can distract her from a target, and others would be well-advised to take a lesson from the master. This child has exquisite tastes and is very discriminating and discerning about her likes and dislikes. One could say this elegant Sheep has real class!

THE HORSE ASCENDANT—TIME OF BIRTH IS BETWEEN 11 A.M. AND 12:59 P.M.

The Horse inspires this Sheep child with the courage to explore new ground and make a game out of the adventure. This type of flamboyant personality attracts the attention of peers, who love to listen to the exciting tales of this Sheep-Horse's travels. A born storyteller, this child can express passionate emotions. This Sheep has the natural inclination to give, like her brethren, while the Horse ascendant is more selfish and chases after what she wants with fierce determination. With the Horse ascendant, this child will not fear taking chances and will have a deep trust in fate and herself. She is likely to change her mind and have quick reactions. Her love of sports and action will distinguish her.

THE SHEEP ASCENDANT—TIME OF BIRTH IS BETWEEN 1 P.M. AND 2:59 P.M.

This child's strengths and weaknesses are one and the same—sensitive and generous to a fault. Sheep grow solid attachments to those they love and fear the very idea of letting go. Working exceptionally well in a group, she will excel in nurturing cooperation. She is the ultimate cheerleader, enjoying the role of supporter rather than that of trailblazer. With the proper mentor, this child may develop the creative talents of the Sheep and spark new independence. She is a gracious and loving soul who works hard at getting along with others, sometimes giving too much of herself and being taken for granted. Still, luck seems to favor her and she always comes out ahead.

THE MONKEY ASCENDANT—TIME OF BIRTH IS BETWEEN 3 P.M. AND 4:59 P.M.

The hyperactive Monkey influence may be the dose of caffeine that this Sheep needs to start off the day. This ascendant donates ingenuity and a very healthy amount of confidence to the modest and reticent Sheep. Both signs are fun-loving and positive, but while the Sheep loves to observe, the Monkey loves to become actively involved and get a piece of the action. This intuitive child will stick her neck out and reap the benefits of the Monkey's keen strategies and the artfulness of the benevolent Sheep—charm and intelligence combined in an irresistible and attractive way. This is a child who knows how to have fun while discovering shortcuts to getting her work done quickly.

THE ROOSTER ASCENDANT—TIME OF BIRTH IS BETWEEN 5 P.M. AND 6:59 P.M.

Two dreamers operate in the mind of this young one—the elaborate visions of the hardworking Rooster and the sweet fantasies of the Sheep. The Rooster ascendant gives order and a trendsetting style to the shy but artistic Sheep. Much can be accomplished if the inner self of a Rooster takes charge while the native Sheep sign tempers out a good balance by not being too critical. With a range from saintly generosity to shameful frugality and nagging, this child has both signs dwelling within her. She will be sharp and calculating but still have a soft spot for those in need.

THE DOG ASCENDANT—TIME OF BIRTH IS BETWEEN 7 P.M. AND 8:59 P.M.

This child will be practical and well respected for such well thought out behavior. The Dog personality has a thick skin and takes critical suggestions in stride. Also naturally street smart, the faithful Dog ascendant helps the Sheep weather any kind of storm and handle everyday obstacles without too much fussing or stress. As a result of her Dog inner self, this Sheep child is able to work independently or with others. This combination brings out the assertiveness of the Dog and the peace-loving kindness and cooperation of the Sheep. This is a friendly and likeable child with her own convictions and astute opinions.

THE BOAR ASCENDANT—TIME OF BIRTH IS BETWEEN 9 P.M. AND 10:59 P.M.

Hurray! The life of the party has arrived. The Boar ascendant's incredible zest for life as well as addiction to food and friends alike infect others quite thoroughly. This Sheep is a friend who is patient, kind, and encouraging. Finding the lighter side of every situation, the Boar weathers hard times with the knowledge that better ones are sure to come. The Sheep can be petulant and changeable and overly sensitive. Thankfully, the tough Boar ascendant gives this Sheep child the emotional support and resolve she needs. Nevertheless, this child's appetite for the rich pleasures of life may need to be curbed, through lessons in finance and self-control.

Famous Persons Born in the Year of the Sheep

Andy Warhol

Barbara Walters

Desmond Tutu

Catherine Deneuve

King George IV

Michelangelo

James Michener

Sir Lawrence Olivier

Ian Smith

George Wallace

Muhammad Ali

Bobby Fischer

John Denver

Isaac Asimov

Mikhail Gorbachev

Andrew Carnegie

Archbishop Fulton Sheen

Rudolph Valentino

Miguel de Cervantes

Nat King Cole

Dino de Laurentiis

Pierre Trudeau

Shah Mohammad Reza Pahlavi

Douglas Fairbanks

Billie Jean King

Arthur Conan Doyle

As a treat to your child, please read the Sheep's story,
"The Three Blessings," which follows.

THE SHEEP'S STORY

"THE THREE BLESSINGS"

When the world was just beginning, animals and humans were friends and could speak to one another quite easily. No one killed or hunted the animals, and humans and all other creatures lived together in peace.

This is the story of a member of the Sheep family whose name was Peony. Not only was this young ewe as lovely as the Queen of Flowers, the peony, but she also got her name because her fleece curled and grew in concentric circles like the petals of the peony blossom.

Needless to say, Peony was very proud of her snowy white fleece and how luxurious and abundant it was. Peony, her siblings, cousins, and flock mates would rub themselves against short thorn branches to rake out dirt from their fleece and to fluff out the wool. Peony had a sweet nature and an easygoing disposition. Like her peers, Peony stayed close to her flock, as Sheep loved the security of family and felt vulnerable away from the group. They ate the abundant grass and grazed on meadow flowers, clovers, and the young leaves of shrubs. Every evening they would stroll down to the river for a long cool drink. The other animals marveled at how the lambs would kneel to suckle from their mothers and often referred to this admirable trait as a symbol of a child's love and respect for its parents' nurturing and love.

Peony's playmates were her favorite cousin, Rosie, and a black Sheep called San-San. The three of them were devoted to one another and could be curious, silly, and irresponsible all at the same time. Rosie was their outspoken leader and knew every bit of gossip there was. San-San was the comedian and would tell all sorts of jokes and do hilarious imitations of other Sheep and animals. Peony and her friends loved adventure and would seek out new things to do and try to spice up their rather protected existence. When all one had to do each day was to chew grass and flowers and take a leisurely walk down to the river before sunset for a long, cool drink, it was easy to become bored, no matter how entertaining the company. Every time the fun-loving trio got bored, Rosie or San-San would think of some new escapade to break the monotony of their lives.

As they grew older, they would wander off to other flocks to exchange news, catch up on the latest gossip, or simply have the excitement of tasting different types of grass. Being extremely sociable, Peony, Rosie, and San-San could make new friends wherever they went. Before long, they became acquainted with the deer tribe. The deer liked the Sheep because they had similar interests and ate the same food, but since the deer were more active by nature, they would often run and jump around and the Sheep could not keep up with the athletic and boisterous deer. The Sheep also befriended the Rabbits, Boars, Dogs, Oxen, and even the Monkeys who communicated expertly with everyone and were very fussy about what kinds of leaves or fruit they would eat. There was no bit of fun or any game that eluded this sociable and outgoing group.

Peony was more loved than the other Sheep in their large and varied circle of friends because she had a kind heart and always believed in the goodness of others. Besides that, she was extremely generous. Peony would listen sympathetically to every hard-luck story—no matter how far-fetched. As a result, she was often taken advantage of and her two friends would chide her.

"You're such a ninny at times, Peony," San-San would scold, "don't believe everything they tell you."

"Yes, you are much too naive and impressionable," Rosie would chime in. "One of these days, you could get into real trouble if we are not here to protect you."

Peony would shrug off their admonitions with a laugh.

"C'mon, girls, I don't mind helping others, even if I am naive at times. We must never lose faith in others, and even if I am the butt of their jokes, it is not in me to turn down anyone who needs my help. There may come a day when someone may really need our help and we would ignore them simply because we are not really sure if they are truly in trouble or just playing some prank."

And so it happened one cold winter day as the entire flock walked down to the river before sunset for their long, cool drink. Peony, Rosie, and San-San always had to find their own clean, uncrowded spot where they could drink slowly and peacefully without interruptions or pushing from other Sheep. Rosie picked a quiet spot downstream that had a few large boulders and some bushes around.

"Here's a nice spot," she called to San-San and Peony, "come over here."

It had snowed the night before and patches of snow and ice were still visible in the pristine area around the river's edge. As the three ewes were drinking, San-San made some witty observations and did an extremely accurate imitation of an old goat. Peony and Rosie had a fit of laughter and they giggled so much, they could hardly drink. As they joked and laughed, they heard a strange, low moan coming from one of the bushes. At first, they thought it was just their imagination; after all, San-San had just made such noises and moans copying the old goat. Then they heard it get louder.

"It's coming from that bush next to the big boulder," Peony said.

"Be careful, Peony, you better let me have a look first," said Rosie protectively.

The three approached cautiously and saw an almost naked old man huddled between the bush and the boulder. He only had a thin piece of undergarment and he was soaking wet and shivering. His hair was dripping with water and his teeth chattered so badly that he could hardly speak.

"Please . . . help me. I'm so . . . so cold," shivered the old man.

"What happened to you, old man?" questioned Rosie.

"I . . . I was trying to cross . . . the . . . the . . . river when I fell in and got washed downstream. I . . . I lost my c-c-cloak, my tunic, sh-sh-shoes, my . . . my purse and even my . . . wa-walking stick," he answered with difficulty.

"We must find a way to warm him and get him some clothes before he freezes to death," San-San said nervously.

But Peony was already pulling off some wool from her shoulders and rubbing herself against the bushes to get more wool off to use for the old man.

"Here, here, you could have some of my wool to warm you, sir," Peony said, as she kept tearing wool off her fleece and handing it to him with her mouth.

"But I am s-s-still so . . . so-o c-c-cold . . . ," replied the freezing man. "I n-n-need your entire fleece to keep m-m-me warm. Would . . . would you s-s-sacrifice your fleece for m-me, kind Sh-Sh-Sheep?"

Rosie and San-San were aghast at the mere thought of such a bold suggestion and opened their mouths to object strongly when Peony moved closer to the poor, shivering man and quietly said, "Yes, I would."

In an instant, Peony's entire fleece fell off and she was left naked while the old man was draped with her beautiful, thick, curly fleece.

San-San and Rosie screamed in unison.

"Oh, no, Peony, look at you! You look ghastly without anything on. Now you've really gone and done it. Have you lost your mind?"

Then a strange and wonderful thing happened. The old man got up and changed into a young monk with a serene smile and strong voice.

"Peony, I am the Lord Buddha. I often come to earth in different guises or reincarnate myself in different forms to test if there is some selfless creature who would come to my aid. You are one who possesses a pure and unselfish heart and did not hesitate to help someone in need. Your sacrifice was not easy to make, and yet you were able to put aside all thoughts of your own welfare in your desire to save an old man from freezing to death. From this day forth, all Sheep will be able to shed their fleece and have it grow back even better than before. Further to this, I shall bless all Sheep with the three most important needs in life: food, shelter, and clothing. You will never be in want and everyone will take care of you. You will be recognized forever for your sacrifice and valued for your kind and loving heart."

With that statement, Peony's fleece grew back instantly and looked better and fluffier than before. Rosie and San-San oohed and aahed and looked on proudly at their friend and finally understood that Peony had proven that compassion was a rare virtue valued highly by the Lord Buddha. Peony proved that a good heart brings good and just rewards. As the three friends turned around again, the Lord Buddha had disappeared into a cloud of incense and the bush that protected him had burst into flowers in the middle of winter.

CHAPTER NINE

THE MONKEY

The Ninth Lunar Sign

The sign of the Monkey

Is the mark of genius.

A brilliant and curious mind

Full of practical ideas.

Constantly seeking answers—

Constantly asking questions—

Yet filled with original ideas and solutions.

The Monkey child is a great innovator,

No obstacles too large nor

Boundaries too far are able to contain

The incomparable Monkey—

The masterful wit of the lunar cycle.

His motto is: **FIRST GAIN MASTERY, THEN CREATE OPPORTUNITIES!**

THE MONKEY'S BRANCH

CHINESE NAME FOR THE MONKEY: *Hóu*

RANK: Ninth

HOURS OF THE MONKEY: From 3 P.M. to 4:59 P.M.*

DIRECTION OF THIS BRANCH: West-southwest

SEASON AND PRINCIPAL MONTH: Summer and August

CORRESPONDS TO THE WESTERN SIGN: Leo, the Lion

FIXED ELEMENT: Metal

STEM: Yang, or masculine

* Ascendant: *Children who are born during the two-hour segment of the day ruled by the Monkey sign will have this sign as their ascendant and will display affinity for people born under this particular sign, as well as have many of the distinct character traits that identify the Monkey sign.*

FIVE CYCLES* OF THE LUNAR YEARS OF THE MONKEY IN THE WESTERN CALENDAR

START DATE		END DATE	ELEMENT OF THE YEAR
January 30, 1968	to	February 16, 1969	Earth
February 16, 1980	to	February 4, 1981	Metal
February 4, 1992	to	January 22, 1993	Water
January 22, 2004	to	February 8, 2005	Wood
February 8, 2016	to	January 27, 2017	Fire

* A cycle on the lunar horoscope equals twelve years. Five cycles completes sixty years.

Note: One who is born on the day before the start of the lunar year of the Monkey, e.g., February 3, 1992, will belong to the animal sign before the Monkey, which is the Sheep, the eighth lunar sign. One who is born on the day after the end of the lunar year of the Monkey, e.g., January 23, 1993, belongs to the animal sign following the Monkey, which is the Rooster, the tenth lunar sign.

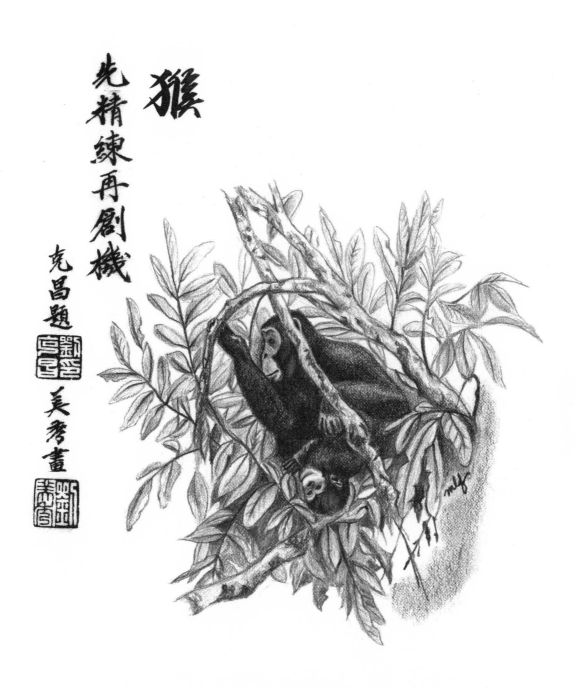

先精練再創機

猴

克昌題

美秀畫

THE MONKEY SIGN

FIRST GAIN MASTERY, THEN CREATE OPPORTUNITIES

The Monkey Personality

The ninth earth branch of the Chinese lunar cycle is named *Shen* and is affectionately known as the Monkey. This is the sign of the quick-witted innovator who loves to be challenged and actively participates in everything around him. The *Shen* personality is a curious and creative child, intelligent and boldly inquisitive. A child born in the year of the *Shen* earth branch needs a lot of mental activity and discipline to contain his competitive nature and make him more cooperative and team oriented. This sign represents creative ideas sparked from a deep curiosity and ingenuity. But such a powerfully gifted child needs direction and guidance. His intricate mind is usually deceptively simple on the surface. He will ask you a few innocent questions and may even have a few funny observations, and then he springs an unbelievably novel theory on you—which is even more remarkable because his deductions were right on the mark and his solution is ingenious and previously undiscovered. Impossible? The Monkey personality loves this word—because he is here to prove it wrong. Shrewd, smart, and nonchalant in his smugness, he strives to outdo and outsmart unbelievers.

Highly social and great at interacting with adults and peers, the often hyperactive Monkey child is precocious and can be quite uninhibited at making his wishes and desires known, and he can be strong-willed and tenacious in having his way. Communication is vital to him, so he learns to talk early and tries to take control of his own little world and that of his parents, too. Here is a personality good at expressing himself and never in doubt about the best way (usually his way) on how to do something.

Children of the ninth branch love eating and learn to appreciate different tastes and textures of food at an early age. They are also easy to teach and love games, and they may invent a few of their own, bending the rules to give themselves the edge. Delightfully adaptable, the Monkey could be the life of the party or the scheming little plotter behind each coup.

This entertaining child will be able to keep track of his possessions and will

develop an early inclination to repair his toys or put together difficult puzzles or devices that could confound even adults. A natural problem solver, he sees things in a different light and depth from others, and his solutions are usually practical and inventive. However, this little storehouse of ideas, shortcuts, and quick fixes may also have a conniving side and will not take no for an answer. He sees everything as challenges that he must conquer and will keep trying until he gets the right combinations or answers.

He also has a suspicious side to his nature, as he always wants to remain number one and can't stand it if anyone should dare to outsmart him. The ambitious Monkey child makes friends easily because he loves group activity and is able to communicate with all kinds of people. Usually he is not shy, but outgoing and even audacious in a happy way. His resourcefulness and assertiveness is refreshing, as he carves his own niche of expertise early in life.

On the other hand, a child of this earth branch can be critical, argumentative, and difficult when he feels oppressed by unfair rules. He can be spontaneous and easygoing, as he is versatile enough to know how to handle himself and be flexible in all kinds of situations. The Monkey child is an opportunist and a strategist who knows how to look out for himself. And, although he may be good at covering up his real intentions, his parents usually catch on to his little tricks soon enough.

Do not underestimate the Monkey's sharpness and ability to understand what is actually going on around him. He knows his own limits and expects to work hard to win recognition based on his own merits. Resolute and self-assured, he has a remarkable memory and strives constantly to improve himself. He prefers not to depend too much on others and tends to act on his own once he finds out all the facts and weighs his options. This personality never accepts things at face value but tends to question, explore, and investigate to his own satisfaction. An extrovert who needs little encouragement or validation from others, the wily and sometimes mischievous Monkey child is a self-starter who will amaze you with his talents and self-confidence.

Birth Order and Sibling Rivalry

*FIRSTBORN OR ONLY CHILD

When the Monkey child is the firstborn or only child, he puts himself under a lot of self-created pressure. He can be quite intense and is a handful for his parents to manage. He learns to communicate early and to communicate well so that he can explain to others why and how things should be done his way. If he is the firstborn or only child, he is able to take center stage and receive the full attention of his parents without any competition until the other children are born. He enjoys his position as the leader and could be bossy and opinionated, but he tries his utmost to live up to and even surpass his parents' high expectations of him. In this birth position, the Monkey is even more an overachiever than normal and sets very high standards for himself. There is a selfish streak in the Monkey, and he may not be good at sharing with younger siblings. At first, he may become shocked at the appearance of a sibling whom he views as a competitor, and then he works even harder to solidify his superior position in the family. It is not enough for the Monkey firstborn to be just ahead—he must be way ahead to feel comfortable that no one will be nipping at his heels.

MIDDLE OR LATER-BORN CHILD

The Monkey as the middle child will be competitive and high-strung because he has to vie for attention from the firstborn. He works hard to dethrone the firstborn, and the only one who would work harder is his twin. The Monkey as the middle child may feel that he is better than the firstborn and tends to challenge his older sibling to prove his own excellence and worthiness. In trying to excel and to ultimately displace the firstborn, the Monkey in the middle position tries to be on equal footing with the firstborn or even get one notch higher. He is able to take responsibility and tends to be domineering when he is in charge.

In order to upgrade himself, he is often jealous of the firstborn and will want to have everything his older sibling has. Very people oriented, the Monkey child

* When a child is born five years after another child, he or she is also considered a firstborn child.

is responsible and interacts well with his peers as well as his teachers. However, he is a protector to younger siblings because he needs support in his battles, so the firstborn and the younger siblings can be manipulated to help him in his little schemes for dominance. Being wedged in as the middle child forces the Monkey in this position to juggle everything furiously to his favor. Thankfully, he will excel in this job and meet all the challenges he places on himself.

YOUNGEST OR LAST-BORN CHILD

The youngest is defined as the younger of two children or the youngest of all the siblings. This is a nice and cozy niche for the Monkey child born in this position. As the baby, he is adored, spoiled, and given more leeway than the older siblings—all of which he will cleverly use to his advantage. This birth position is a low-stress position, as everyone expects less of the baby and tends to make excuses for his shortcomings. But instead of basking in his family's adoration, the competitive Monkey as the last born tends to hide his ambitions and tenacity and quietly but surely takes advantage of all presented opportunities. Before the family knows it, this seemingly sweet and obedient Monkey "baby" will be the millionaire in the family.

Ascendants

In Chinese horoscopes, the two-hour segment ruling the time of birth is known as the ascendant sign. This can also be referred to as the child's "inner self."

The time of birth used to determine the ascendant is always the local time in the place of birth.

For a child born in the Year of the Monkey:

THE RAT ASCENDANT—TIME OF BIRTH IS BETWEEN 11 P.M. AND 12:59 A.M.

Others will naturally gravitate to this dynamic child born with the Rat ascendant, and they will not be disappointed. In addition to being a gifted conversationalist and host, he knows the true meaning of friendship. This sentimental child likes to surround himself with trusted people and will fill his life with all sorts of friends and family. Not afraid to mix public and personal affairs, he might even prefer to work with loved ones. This charming Monkey is sociable, generous, and knows how to take care of himself while remaining popular and well regarded. With the Rat as his inner self, this particular Monkey child is gifted with eloquence, good judgment, and an affectionate nature, especially when he wants something badly.

THE OX ASCENDANT—TIME OF BIRTH IS BETWEEN 1 A.M. AND 2:59 A.M.

With the Ox as his ascendant, this child is less spontaneous than other Monkeys. Cautious and dependable, he works more by the tried and true method of the disciplined Ox than by feelings and hunches. Not as outspoken or unconventional as other Monkeys, he favors rules and excels in matters of detail and organization. Not surprisingly, this combination produces some excellent scholars and teachers. This child has high expectations of himself as well as of others. The disciplined Ox makes him take the straight and narrow path instead of the shortcuts. The trade-off is extremely fair because Monkeys always deliver, and this child is true to his word.

THE TIGER ASCENDANT—TIME OF BIRTH IS BETWEEN 3 A.M. AND 4:59 A.M.

With the colorful Tiger as his ascendant, this child will be outgoing, adventurous and very charming. Definitely one to learn by experience, he is least likely to be consulting any outside advice. With the unpredictable Tiger as his inner self, this captivating and energetic Monkey does have trouble making up his mind. Besides being dramatic and even theatrical in his desire to stay in the limelight, this Monkey could be prone to changing his mind often. He is excitable and wants to sample everything at the buffet. Usually such adventures end up with a tummy ache and a lot of moaning.

On the whole, the Tiger and Monkey combination here produces a vivacious child brimming over with personality and many talents. If he can harness his natural energy and focus, there is no stopping this kid.

THE RABBIT ASCENDANT—TIME OF BIRTH IS BETWEEN 5 A.M. AND 6:59 A.M.

The Rabbit ascendant gives the Monkey a leading edge, with its intuitive ways and keen judgment. Like most Monkeys, this child will be enterprising and talented, and, most important, he knows how to hold his tongue. With a kind and responsible ascendant such as this one, he is able to get into the good graces of anyone, despite the underlying mischievous ways of the Monkey. Others will seek this child out for guidance, decisions, or even matters of taste. This is a quiet, clever, and sagacious Monkey, who looks angelic but is way ahead of any game. Don't be fooled, he plays to win.

THE DRAGON ASCENDANT—TIME OF BIRTH IS BETWEEN 7 A.M. AND 8:59 A.M.

Gifted with vision and an overwhelming amount of optimism, this child with the Dragon ascendant could go out and achieve most anything he sets his mind and heart to. The Dragon ascendant contributes a wealth of energy to the already powerful and inventive Monkey. He will enjoy doing things on a grand scale, to try to match the elaborate ways of his egotistic mind. Friends and strangers alike are taken by his infectious enthusiasm and never-say-die attitude. This child has fans and followers at every turn. He could summon up an army when he needs help.

THE SNAKE ASCENDANT—TIME OF BIRTH IS BETWEEN 9 A.M. AND 10:59 A.M.

The veritable Snake is a valuable accomplice to the Monkey's master plan. Others can marvel at how this child will be able to tempt and persuade others without giving anything away. The Snake ascendant makes this Monkey child inscrutable and secretive. The Monkey's innate ability to get whatever he wants comes from charm, intelligence, and a healthy dose of discretion that may be enhanced by having the Snake as his inner self. While this child may be very outgoing, much of who he really is lies locked away deep inside. There is no forcing anything out of this child; he prefers to act when ready and not a moment before.

THE HORSE ASCENDANT—TIME OF BIRTH IS BETWEEN 11 A.M. AND 12:59 P.M.

With the Horse sign as his ascendant, this confident and strong-willed child will not be one to back down from anything he truly believes in. The adventurous Horse is prone to acting upon emotions and impulse. Fortunately, the brainy Monkey knows how to look at things with a more practical and realistic eye and forces the Horse inner self to bide his time. Together, this combination produces a creative and innovative problem solver who loves fast action and sports but is also sensible and intelligent.

THE SHEEP ASCENDANT—TIME OF BIRTH IS BETWEEN 1 P.M. AND 2:59 P.M.

An introspective artist is sure to come out of this combination of Sheep and Monkey. Sympathetic and playful, this Monkey will show his ingenuity in many ways that will positively influence or benefit others. With the thoughtful Sheep as his inner self, here is a compassionate and imaginative Monkey child who will be less selfish and motivated to take up a variety of creative outlets, possibly music, art, or writing. The sociable Monkey and his Sheep ascendant are communications experts and will enjoy the company of many friends. This child's personality is sensitive and caring and he will excel working with and counseling others. While emotions can sometimes override logic, the Monkey's practicality can handle the damage control.

THE MONKEY ASCENDANT—TIME OF BIRTH IS BETWEEN 3 P.M. AND 4:59 P.M.

This pure Monkey child enjoys competition and happily performs on any stage that welcomes him. Monkey children with the same sign as their ascendant are talented magicians and enjoy any challenge that life tosses at them. Part of this child's idealistic view of life comes from the ease in which everything seems to come to him. He will enjoy confronting and taming situations that others may shy away from. This proactive child will find pleasure in creating opportunities for himself, for he is ambitious and loves unraveling a good mystery.

THE ROOSTER ASCENDANT—TIME OF BIRTH IS BETWEEN 5 P.M. AND 6:59 P.M.

With the Rooster as his ascendant, this child is smart, diligent, and enchanting. The efficiency of the Rooster is enhanced by the superior mental prowess of the gifted Monkey. A captivating speaker and witty little detective, this Monkey child is perceptive and reactive to the extreme. He is cool, collected, and up to any challenge that comes before him. Lucky are the parents who are blessed with this splendid Monkey child. One has to wake up very early in order to pull anything on this little Monkey! He doesn't miss a trick in the book.

THE DOG ASCENDANT—TIME OF BIRTH IS BETWEEN 7 P.M. AND 8:59 P.M.

This is a down-to-earth Monkey who can appraise situations with the just and objective eye. With a Dog ascendant, this child will not be afraid of working hard if he knows that the end is worth fighting for. Enjoying the simpler things in life, he finds peace in calm and easy living with the Dog as his inner self. While typically reserved and fair minded, when he is stirred by injustice, this Monkey is quick to act and act with conviction. Friends are indeed fortunate to have this Monkey in their corner. This child is a creative doer who has no qualms standing up for his rights and no dilemmas about doing the right thing at the right time.

THE BOAR ASCENDANT—TIME OF BIRTH IS BETWEEN 9 P.M. AND 10:59 P.M.

With a Boar ascendant, this child will be generous and aims to please those he loves. It will be a delight to work with such a cooperative and kind Monkey. He will indulge in life's pleasures and encourage those around him to take part in the fun. Tomorrow will take care of itself. With the passionate Boar as his inner self, the Monkey is strong and fearless as well as an apt pupil who does not fear hard work or sacrifice. Persons close to this child will value his warmth and honesty. He will surely have a wonderful reputation of fortitude, cooperation, and charity. This particular child is not as selfish as other Monkeys and has a lot more friends and admirers.

Famous Persons Born in the Year of the Monkey

Harry Truman

Eleanor Roosevelt

Walter Matthau

Mario Puzo

Pope John Paul II

Julius Caesar

Elizabeth Taylor

Charles Dickens

Joan Crawford

Bette Davis

Duchess of Windsor

Queen Sirikit of Thailand

John Milton

Paul Gauguin

Martina Navratilova

Diana Ross

Harry Houdini

Nelson Rockefeller

Edward Kennedy

Mujibur Rahman

Lyndon B. Johnson

Mick Jagger

Milton Berle

Jack Nicklaus

As a treat to your child, please read the Monkey's story,
"The Legend of the Monkey King," which follows.

148

T
H
E

M
O
N
K
E
Y

THE MONKEY'S STORY

"THE LEGEND OF THE MONKEY KING"

No one really knows when the Monkey King was born or exactly where he came from. It is said that he was born from a large stone egg high above a mountain, so high it reached the heavens. It was called Hua Kuo San, the Mountain of Flowers and Fruits. The sun's warmth nurtured the stone egg, and the four winds and the clouds and mists kept watch over it. One day during a violent storm, a single fiery bolt of lightning struck it and cracked it open. Out popped a golden life-size Monkey with five keen senses and full-grown limbs.

All the immortals in the heavens were aware of his strange birth, and at first they called him the Stone Monkey. However, the Stone Monkey proved himself to be very capable and intelligent and he made Hua Kuo San his home. His fame attracted many other Monkeys and their cousins to join him on his beautiful mountain so close to the sky. The Stone Monkey then presided over a growing kingdom of Monkeys, Chimpanzees, Gorillas, Marmosets, Orangutans, and every possible Monkey cousin there was. They all loved their strong leader and lived quite happily in their mountain full of flowers and fruit.

As the Stone Monkey accumulated more and more followers, he began to hear of many abuses committed against the Monkey population. How many of his subjects were kidnapped and forced to work for humans and perform circus tricks, or taught to become pickpockets and to steal and do other terrible things against their will. Finally, the Stone Monkey, who was now proclaimed as the Monkey King, decided to do something about these deplorable acts committed against his people. Now, as you know, the Monkey's kingdom extended all the way up to the back door of the heavens as it reached into the sky. So the Monkey King had no difficulty knowing where the gods lived and where to go to lodge an official complaint on the ill treatment of Monkeys everywhere.

However, he picked a day on which all the immortals were having a celebration for an important event, all gathered in the banquet hall. The Monkey King did not know this, so when he could not find anyone to receive him, he felt free to wander around the gardens looking for someone to tell him where to go. He wandered into a secluded and lovely garden, where he found an exquisitely beautiful peach tree laden with ripe fruit. Little did he know these were the Peaches of Immortality, which only grew and ripened once in a thousand years. Being one who loved peaches and fruits of any kind, the Monkey King helped himself to the heavenly peaches and was so surprised at how good they tasted (and he was used to the best of everything). All of a sudden, he heard a lady scream and the next thing he knew he was surrounded by fierce guards and arrested. Imagine the horror of the Queen of Heaven at being told by her attendants that a huge Monkey invaded her heavenly garden and ate her priceless peaches. The Monkey King was brought before all the immortals for judgment. No one was interested in listening to his complaints or how he got lost and found his way into the Queen's celestial garden. Everyone in the heavens was extremely angry with the Monkey King. They called him a horrible thief and a bandit of the lowest kind and sentenced him to death. Of course, they quickly realized that they could not even kill him, because he became an immortal like them after eating the heavenly peaches. The Monkey King saw the predicament of the greater and lesser gods, and since he had a wonderful sense of humor, he started laughing at the situation. This lack of respect made the gods even angrier and more determined to punish him and teach him to mind his manners and know his place.

"Is this the Stone Monkey born from a rock egg?" they asked one another arrogantly.

"He has no parents except the Sun and the Moon, who watched over him because they have nothing better to do, and that accounts for his total lack of manners in the presence of his superiors," complained another celestial being.

"We cannot keep him here with us," whispered a young goddess, hiding behind the Queen of Heaven, "he looks so dangerous and tricky . . . and . . . and . . . what if he escapes?"

"I agree," said a lesser god, "and who knows what other schemes and calamities could happen with this uncivilized creature in our midst. Calling himself the King of the Monkeys, indeed!"

"We have no choice," said the Jade Emperor, "we must imprison the Monkey King in the Realm of the Underworld for his crime."

So the Monkey King was escorted to the Underworld in chains by the mighty warrior god, Erh Lang, who rode on his black steed and was accompanied by his faithful hound. Once they reached the underworld, there were thirty-three levels of Hell (as compared to only seven levels of Heaven). However, in order for one to be processed in the Underworld, his name had to be registered in the Registry of Death. Somehow, the Monkey King's faithful followers had learned of his misfortune and journeyed to the Underworld to set their leader free. No doubt they went through much hardship and obstacles, but the Monkey King's followers were reunited with their beloved leader.

Once he was freed, the Monkey King quickly got hold of the Registry of Death and tore out the pages that contained his name and the names of his friends and comrades. This clever act was a clear victory over death, as everyone knows that if your name is not in the Death Registry, then you simply can't die. By now, the Monkey King had achieved "double immortality" (if that is at all possible) and became truly indestructible. His escape was viewed with the gravest concern by all heavenly beings, but his followers were overjoyed with having him back and they all returned to the Mountain of Flowers and Fruits in triumph.

Still, the heavenly beings persisted in exacting their justice upon the Monkey King, who thwarted all their efforts to subdue or control him. By now, the Monkey King had accumulated some awesome powers of his own. He had mastered the art of "cloud jumping" and could leap to a distance of 36,000 meters with his magical sandals, and he could change himself into seventy-two different forms. As a weapon against his enemies, he carried a gold-capped pole that he obtained from the Dragon King; it would grow to his height when he commanded. This gold-capped pole would shrink to the size of a toothpick when not in use and he would hide it behind his ear. When the odds were against him in battle, he would pluck hairs from his chest and with a powerful spell conjure up followers to fight with him. Each hair would change into an exact replica or clone of the Monkey King, so it was hard to know which one was the original, since there were so many duplicates.

After 350 years had passed and the Monkey King's fur had turned pure white from age, the immortals decided it was time to end their long struggle with the Monkey King. He had achieved the level of a sage, an enlightened being, and had earned some respect. However, they ordered him on an impossible mission to recover the Holy Scriptures of Buddha, which had been stolen. His ordeal was recorded in a long novel called *Journey to the West*. The Monkey King was able to accomplish his mission to the ends of the earth and beyond and recovered the Holy Scriptures for the Jade Emperor of Heaven.

After he had accomplished all his impossible missions, his name was changed to Sun Wu-K'ung by the monk who ordained him and journeyed with him to the West. As he had shown great discipline and perseverance and moral uprightness in fulfilling his promises, the Jade Emperor was forced to keep his end of the bargain and elevate Sun Wu-K'ung to the rank of sainthood. The Monkey King was officially made a god and awarded the prestigious title "Great Sage Equal to Heaven." In reality, all the immortals were so vexed with him that to this day they still call him (behind his back, of course) the "Great Pain in the Neck Equal to None." Upon being presented with this immense honor, the Monkey King, now the Monkey God, returned to his own kingdom, where he ruled wisely, keeping his promise not to plague the other gods with his tricks nor match wits with any of the immortals.

Every year on the twenty-third day of the second lunar moon, everyone celebrates the Monkey God's birthday, and Monkeys everywhere say a prayer for their famous leader and ask for his protection.

CHAPTER TEN

THE ROOSTER

The Tenth Lunar Sign

The Rooster is the meticulous Timekeeper

Of the lunar cycle.

She thrives on clockwork and precision.

A capable and efficient administrator,

The Rooster takes pride in her appearance and performance

And will not overlook the smallest detail.

Full of grandiose ambitions and

High-flying ideas—

This colorful and controversial personality

Achieves success at the most mundane of endeavors.

Yet, the dauntless Rooster pursues a constant

Quest for order and perfection in her universe.

Her motto is: **ONE SINGS, ALL WILL FOLLOW**

THE ROOSTER'S BRANCH

CHINESE NAME FOR THE ROOSTER: $\overline{Ji}$

RANK: Tenth

HOURS OF THE ROOSTER: From 5 P.M. to 6:59 P.M.*

DIRECTION OF THIS BRANCH: Directly west

SEASON AND PRINCIPAL MONTH: Autumn and September

CORRESPONDS TO THE WESTERN SIGN: Virgo, the Virgin

FIXED ELEMENT: Metal

STEM: Yin, feminine

* Ascendant: *Children who are born during the two-hour segment of the day ruled by the Rooster sign will have this sign as their ascendant and will display affinity for people born under this particular sign, as well as have many of the distinct character traits that identify the Rooster sign.*

FIVE CYCLES* OF THE LUNAR YEARS OF THE ROOSTER IN THE WESTERN CALENDAR

START DATE		END DATE	ELEMENT OF THE YEAR
February 17, 1969	to	February 5, 1970	Earth
February 5, 1981	to	January 24, 1982	Metal
January 23, 1993	to	February 9, 1994	Water
February 9, 2005	to	January 28, 2006	Wood
January 28, 2017	to	February 5, 2018	Fire

* A cycle on the lunar horoscope equals twelve years. Five cycles completes sixty years.

Note: One who is born on the day before the start of the lunar year of the Rooster, e.g., January 22, 1993, will belong to the animal sign before the Rooster, which is the Monkey, the ninth lunar sign. One who is born on the day after the end of the lunar year of the Rooster, e.g., February 10, 1994, belongs to the animal sign following the Rooster, which is the Dog, the eleventh lunar sign.

THE ROOSTER SIGN
ONE SINGS, ALL WILL FOLLOW

The Rooster Personality

The tenth earth branch of the Chinese lunar cycle is named *You* and symbolized by the popular Rooster, or Chicken, sign. In China, the *You* branch is also called the Cock or Cockerel. The *You* branch is a sign of tenacity, and likewise a child born in its year will display the characteristic traits of diligence, perseverance, and industriousness. The Rooster personality will display a sense of purpose and organization in everything she does early in life. She tends to be methodical and consistent and is a creature of habit.

A little self-starter, the Rooster child is a quick learner and the most industrious of all the twelve animal signs. To put it simply, she loves work. She must keep busy. The Rooster enjoys cataloging her toys and possessions, making little charts and ledgers for her real or imaginary stocks and bonds, and other accounting and bookkeeping exercises to see that everything is in order and accounted for. To her, this is not work. Some Roosters may even look at it as a form of relaxation. In real life, of course, she can be most impractical. What appears perfect on paper does not always make sense in practice. And this is one area where the Rooster must learn to understand reality. This little bird has the uncanny knack for putting complicated things in order, but also for making simple things complicated by overzealous meddling.

Optimistic by nature, at times she can be impractical and overbearing. The Rooster child always has a plan and a backup plan and yet another backup plan. Do you see why she is so complicated in her outlook? She wants everything to be in perfect order and will not hesitate to rearrange everything she can get her hands on: the furniture, the budget, your schedule, computer programs, the menu, ad infinitum. Here is someone who does not hesitate to speak her mind and she usually has all the facts on hand to back her arguments. But in spite of her being demanding, critical, and even eccentric in her little obsessions, she is the most pure-minded and helpful child around. She can be depended on to check facts and confirm and reconfirm schedules and information that everyone takes for granted. Her research and findings will usually be impeccable and she will be an outstanding student in whatever field she is interested. You can rely on her to investigate a mystery to the bitter end like a modern-day Sherlock Holmes. No detail, no matter how minute, escapes her attention. She will leave no stone unturned.

Gifted with tremendous energy and zeal, the intellectual Rooster has a flair for influencing others. She may be very quiet at one extreme or very noisy when her feathers are ruffled, but she is great at analyzing things and speaking her mind with eloquence.

Birth Order and Sibling Rivalry

*FIRSTBORN OR ONLY CHILD

The Rooster child is the original Dad's or Mom's indispensable little helper in this birth position. Diligent, self-reliant, and confident, this firstborn or only child is not a crybaby and knows early in life that she is head of the barnyard. She takes her elevated status very seriously, of course, and tends to be a bit cock-sure, especially when she is acting with the authority vested in her by Mom or Dad. Yet she is caring and protective in many ways and will take the younger siblings under her wing and even do their homework for them. Conscientious and responsible, she will have a take-charge attitude and is an excellent role model. Yet she tends to blame herself when something goes wrong and will worry and lecture and remind everyone in the family of their chores and responsibilities. It is hard to fault such a tireless and efficient worker, and one could hardly help but admire the Rooster child, who is really hardest on herself.

MIDDLE OR LATER-BORN CHILD

The Rooster child born in the second or middle position must show even more stamina and fortitude than anyone born before her. This particular child is

---

* When a child is born five years after another child, he or she is also considered a firstborn child.

more assertive and demanding because she craves to be the apple of her parents' eye and would secretly like to direct the eldest on his duties and responsibilities. If the firstborn sibling should fail in any way, this little chick feels more than capable of stepping up and taking over. She realizes this and she prepares for it. The Rooster child in the middle makes herself indispensable in every way, and little by little, she hopes to usurp the number-one position by having her parents and teachers depend more and more on her. She does feel great empathy for her younger brothers and sisters and is inclined to help them follow her path to success. Although her parents may not exert great pressure on her, the Rooster child born in this position will take it upon herself to push herself relentlessly to outshine the firstborn.

YOUNGEST OR LAST-BORN CHILD

This is a difficult position for the Rooster to be in. She longs for more responsibility and wants to be taken seriously by the older ones and her parents. She longs for power and leadership, which is hard to get when one is the baby of the family. As a result, Rooster children in this slot tend to become eccentric and argumentative. Or they will compensate by fashioning their own private world filled with rules and restrictions and be an elitist who bans others from entry into this private universe where she is the absolute ruler. The Rooster will display her independence in this position and will show maturity and efficiency in taking care of herself. She is a self-reliant little soldier who marches to her own drumbeat.

Ascendants

In Chinese horoscopes, the two-hour segment ruling the time of birth is known as the ascendant sign. This can also be referred to as the child's "inner self."

The time of birth used to determine the ascendant is always the local time in the place of birth.

For a child born in the Year of the Rooster:

THE RAT ASCENDANT—TIME OF BIRTH IS BETWEEN 11 P.M. AND 12:59 A.M.
Having the Rat as her ascendant makes this little Rooster a joy to spend time with. This child is highly social and always excited to learn new things. The charming Rat encourages the Rooster to turn heated debates into pleasant discussions and learning experiences. Her peers will seek out this bright child for advice and friendship. But being in this position of counselor for others makes it strange for her when challenged. Still, the highly disciplined Rooster self is critical and picky and finds it hard to ever say she is wrong or admit defeat. The Rat as the inner self is much more practical and would be crafty in protecting her own interests. She will be a passionate student, taking pride in achieving her potential through hard work and attention to details.

THE OX ASCENDANT—TIME OF BIRTH IS BETWEEN 1 A.M. AND 2:59 A.M.
The Ox ascendant encourages the Rooster child to be patient and find the pleasure in taking one step at a time instead of having lofty plans that are difficult to execute. Responsibility will find this child early, and if it doesn't, she will find it. Roosters enjoy managing their finances, so she may enjoy budgeting her weekly allowance or helping around the house to earn some extra money. With the cautious and dependable Ox as her inner self, this child will make few errors and even less false moves. No doubt, this child will be very dependable and organized with a competitive nature. She will like to be punctual and well prepared in all her plans and expects others to be the same way.

THE TIGER ASCENDANT—TIME OF BIRTH IS BETWEEN 3 A.M. AND 4:59 A.M.
The Rooster's nature for order and detail could be trumped by the overpowering nature of the Tiger's love for controversy and spontaneous action. This could result in a short attention span and a child that is interested in a wide variety of topics. Confident and unabashedly charming, this little Rooster makes friends effortlessly. She has an active imagination and a sunny view of the

world. The Tiger as the inner self expects the world to revolve around her, and the Rooster also has a high opinion of herself. A very confident and able performer and student, she is also vocal about likes and dislikes. If she loves you, she will expect you to argue with her and then kiss and make up every time.

THE RABBIT ASCENDANT—TIME OF BIRTH IS BETWEEN 5 A.M. AND 6:59 A.M.

For the discriminating Rooster personality, being born with the Rabbit ascendant is like being educated at a first-rate finishing school. This child will know how to act like a little lady while her clever commentary runs at lightning speed. This Rooster will be quite intelligent and knows how to systematically work toward goals. With the Rabbit as her inner self, she can easily work well with others, with a sweet and sincere personality, while still keeping tabs on everyone. The Rabbit also contributes superb judgment and discretion, which helps curb the sharp tongue of the Rooster. Things could get done without too much rhetoric, and this Rooster child will not leave bruised egos wherever she goes.

THE DRAGON ASCENDANT—TIME OF BIRTH IS BETWEEN 7 A.M. AND 8:59 A.M.

With the domineering Dragon as an ascendant, this Rooster child can be overconfident and overbearing with the very best of intentions. She is a very defined personality with fixed views and strong likes and dislikes. The Dragon brings great strength of character and she will never back down or keep silent if she has an opinion, and she always does. Yet both signs here respect authority and tradition and will fulfill their duties with great dedication. She may not let anyone break or even bend the rules, but she will be a shining example of perfect compliance and probably already has memorized the rule book or even helped to write it.

THE SNAKE ASCENDANT—TIME OF BIRTH IS BETWEEN 9 A.M. AND 10:59 A.M.

With the enigmatic Snake as her ascendant, this Rooster is wise and cautious with her tongue. Studious, reflective, and efficient, she is tenacious and purposeful. On the outside, the Rooster is resplendent and self-confident, but on the inside, she tends to worry, ponder over imaginary problems, and prod for impossible solutions. With the Snake as her inner self, hopefully, she will be more practical and less of a martyr. This Rooster child will have a serene and refined nature and be well behaved because she sees herself as a role model for other children. She is dependable and deeply introspective at times.

THE HORSE ASCENDANT—TIME OF BIRTH IS BETWEEN 11 A.M. AND 12:59 P.M.

The Horse ascendant does the Rooster personality good. The carefree but practical Horse ascendant makes this Rooster less serious and more fun loving. With the Horse as her inner self, this child will be able to do her work and enjoy herself, too, without feeling guilty, as her Rooster half often does. All work and no play makes Jill a dull girl, and this personality is anything but dull! The Horse in her will take shortcuts and improvise without losing a step, while the Rooster half will organize and research facts to everyone's satisfaction. Because both signs are outspoken and quick to criticize, this Rooster reacts aggressively when challenged but is also more flexible and adaptable than other Roosters.

THE SHEEP ASCENDANT—TIME OF BIRTH IS BETWEEN 1 P.M. AND 2:59 P.M.

The Sheep ascendant certainly will provide the Rooster with better manners and a sweeter disposition. She may not be as hardworking, but she will also be less critical and domineering. She is an amiable and less assertive Rooster who wins friends easily because she is so helpful and sympathetic. With the Sheep as guardian of her inner self, this Rooster child is compassionate and not as outspoken as other Roosters. She is a child who appreciates teamwork and works well with others. She may still be particular and detail oriented, but she will strive to encourage others with her excellent example instead of forcing them to toe the line.

THE MONKEY ASCENDANT—TIME OF BIRTH IS BETWEEN 3 P.M. AND 4:59 P.M.

On top of having all the facts and documentation to always prove herself right, this Rooster will have the Monkey's brains to be inventive and crafty, too. Charming, flexible, and capable of changing abruptly to outsmart any competi-

THE

ROOSTER

tion, the Monkey ascendant makes this Rooster very creative and adept. The controlling Rooster ego is made successful and congenial by the Monkey's social skills and love of good strategy. This is a resourceful child who will definitely be an overachiever. Both signs here are hardworking and driven by high standards that they tend to impose on themselves. This particular Rooster's innovative and purposeful outlook will make her constantly on the lookout for good opportunities to pursue and challenges to excel in.

THE ROOSTER ASCENDANT—TIME OF BIRTH IS BETWEEN 5 P.M. AND 6:59 P.M.

A double Rooster sign means this child possesses twice the meticulous attention to details and efficiency of the critical Rooster personality. A double dose of the same industrious and hardworking inclinations could also make this Rooster eccentric and particular in little things. She sticks to her own schedule and hates disruptions or changes—no matter what. Although she is pure-minded, sincere, very helpful, and informed, she can be narrow-minded and unbending when she has made up her mind to do things her way. Tough and unyielding, she deals with problems and opposition in a methodical way, one step at a time. And guess what? Her tenacity and devotion pay off. She will most likely be voted best student in the class.

THE DOG ASCENDANT—TIME OF BIRTH IS BETWEEN 7 P.M. AND 8:59 P.M.

With the Dog guarding the inner self of this Rooster child, she could still be calculating and serious in her outlook, but she will be fair and reasonable. The Dog will listen and reserve judgment until all the evidence is in. The Rooster is of the same idealistic mind but adds color with her salty opinions and argumentative approach. Although the likeable Rooster is loyal and courageous, she may be militant and opinionated when criticized. With the Dog ascendant, this Rooster child is able to have more realistic aspirations and is more practical and warm in her approach. As a result, she will have more friends who will seek her company and enjoy her sharp but witty love of debate. This is a little critic with a noble conscience who really loves to be liked without actually showing it.

THE BOAR ASCENDANT—TIME OF BIRTH IS BETWEEN 9 P.M. AND 10:59 P.M.

The Boar ascendant brings forth a generous and fun-loving Rooster who is popular and great at making friends and organizing charitable events. No one could outdo her in bringing people together and in promoting and marketing her ideas. The diligent Rooster characteristics combined with the earthy power and fortitude of the unselfish Boar will enable this Rooster to go far in achieving her lofty ambitions. Both signs here are energetic but tend to be scrupulous, although the Rooster half certainly worries more than the indulgent Boar inner self. Exacting and driven, this particular Rooster is not as good as other Roosters in handling her own finances as she does find it hard at times to deny her huge appetite for luxury and self-gratification. She does give a lot of herself, but she expects to get a lot back, too.

Famous Persons Born in the Year of the Rooster

Prince Philip

Alex Haley

John Glenn

Barbara Taylor Bradford

King Birendra of Nepal

Errol Flynn

Johann Strauss

Nancy Reagan

Queen Juliana of the Netherlands

Katharine Hepburn

Richard Wagner

Enrico Caruso

Pope Paul IV

Emperor Akihito of Japan

Peter Ustinov

Deborah Kerr

Steve Martin

Dolly Parton

Joan Collins

Edwin Land

Baron Guy de Rothschild

Peter Drucker

Elia Kazan

Somerset Maugham

Daniel K. Ludwig

Grover Cleveland

D. H. Lawrence

As a treat to your child, please read the Rooster's story,
"How the Rooster Got His Comb," which follows.

THE ROOSTER'S STORY

A long, long time ago, just about the time after the world really began, the Rooster and his best friend, the Dragon, were constant companions. They spent their days flying around in the skies with fancy diving stunts to chase each other around. The Rooster then was much bigger than the Peacock, his first cousin, but smaller than the majestic Phoenix, who was also his cousin, from his mother's side. These four friends traveled over all land and waters and mountains.

The Rooster had very plain brown feathers then, and so did the Peacock and the Phoenix, but one day the Dragon showed them how to fly to the end of the rainbow and dip their feathers into the paint bowls of the rainbow immediately after a spring rain. From that time on, the Rooster's feathers and those of his cousins shone like gems with all the colors of the rainbow in them. The Phoenix and the Peacock were prettier than the Rooster, but the Rooster had a beautiful pair of horns and a much lovelier voice. He could sing and crow and reach high notes that his cousins could not. The Rooster took the lead in singing groups and loved to make loud announcements for the entire group. He was delighted to be the master of ceremonies.

The Rooster's horns were not pointed at the tip, but were sort of flat and looked more like two small pronged antlers. The Rooster was proud of his horns because they stood out in a crowd, especially when he was on stage. His best friend, the Dragon, had a red comb, which was really a bit small for him, but this comb was made of rubies and was a gift from the King of Heaven. The Dragon wore it proudly everywhere he went; it didn't hurt to be connected with royalty.

These four friends loved to go to parties and often the Dragon would let the Rooster and the Peacock ride on his back because they could not fly as fast or as far as the Dragon and the Phoenix. It was always fun because the Rooster was an excellent entertainer and would tell wonderful stories and sing ballads for his friends. They had many adventures together and got invited to all the best parties above and below the skies and on both sides of the rainbow bridge.

Then one day, the Dragon was invited to a special party way up in the heavens, and the invitation specified that everyone attending had to wear horns. The Dragon thought about telling the others about the "horns only" party, but then he realized that he did not have any horns. The only one who had any horns was the Rooster. The more the Dragon thought about this, the more he wanted to go to that party. But he realized that if he showed his invitation to the Horn Party to the Rooster, the Rooster would be the only one who could go.

So, instead, the Dragon told the Rooster how much he admired the Rooster's horns and asked if he could borrow them just for a couple of days. The Rooster was flattered but he was also very smart and had never let anyone borrow his precious horns. However, he secretly admired the Dragon's ruby comb and thought that it was way too small for the Dragon, although no one had ever dared to tell the Dragon so. The Rooster suggested that they trade the horns for the comb just for a few days, because it was unfair for the Dragon to wear both while the Rooster did not have anything on his head. The deal was struck and the Dragon wore the Rooster's horns and went to the party alone.

Actually, the horns looked much better on the Dragon than they did on the Rooster, and the Dragon had a roaring time at the Horn Party. Everyone praised his beautiful pair of horns and invited him to more parties. The Dragon became more popular and dignified looking with his new horns than he was before. In the meanwhile, the Dragon's comb fitted the Rooster's smaller head much better than it did the Dragon. The Rooster strutted around with the beautiful red comb and all the animals complimented him. He would perch on top of the fence or even go up to the roof of any house to show off his red comb. When he sang solo, as he often did, the comb stayed on and did not fall off as the horns would do when he shook his head too much.

A week went by and then another and another. The Rooster became worried about his horns and wondered aloud to himself: "Where is my friend, the Dragon? Why has he not returned with my horns?" Early each morning, the

Rooster climbed to the highest point he could find and started crowing: "Dragon, Dragon, give me back my horns! Please give me back my horns!" The word for horns in Chinese sounded like "cock," so when the Rooster crowed "cock-a-doodle-do" at daybreak and at dusk, he was really calling the Dragon to bring back the horns.

As time went by, the horns grew into the Dragon's head just above his eyebrows and felt like a true part of the Dragon's head. The Dragon felt that the horns were his and he would never part with them. He did not miss his ruby comb anymore and came to understand that the comb was way too small for his large head, anyway. In the Dragon's way of looking at things, he and the Rooster did an even trade and the ruby comb was a fair exchange for the horns.

The Rooster, however, missed his horns, although he loved the comb, which had become a part of him, too. The red comb sat up very straight atop the Rooster's head and started growing and extending down his chin and under his beak. It made the Rooster look elegant and imposing. But the Rooster still thought about his lovely pair of horns and just could not believe that his friend the Dragon did not come back to return them. The Rooster would wake up very early each morning, fly to the highest point he could find, and call out to the Dragon to return the horns. Of course, we know the Dragon could not hear him, as he was up in the heavens, having been appointed as Minister of the Rains by the Lord of the Heavens, and had many duties to keep him busy and official functions to attend. The four friends did not meet again, as each went their separate ways. The Rooster became King of the Barnyard and ruled his little kingdom with his loud voice and bright, colorful personality.

There are some who believe that the Rooster is up at the crack of dawn to wake Father Sun and complain about the Dragon and his lost horns. But, as we know, each morning Father Sun greets the Rooster in return with a big smile and says, "Have a lovely day!"

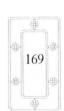

169

THE

ROOSTER'S

STORY

CHAPTER ELEVEN

THE DOG

The Eleventh Lunar Sign

The loyal Dog personality is the

Guardian of the twelve earth branches.

A stalwart protector, the Dog is

Realistic and brave.

His vision is clear and he strives to

Stand up for the truth and the weak.

Yet at heart he is a pacifist, who

Fights only when he sees no other way out.

A champion of just causes who

Values honor and integrity.

The Dog personality is the

Warm and courageous

Defender of the lunar cycle.

His motto is: **JUST AS FAME MUST BE WON, HONOR MUST NOT BE LOST!**

THE DOG'S BRANCH

CHINESE NAME FOR THE DOG: *Gou*

RANK: Eleventh

HOURS OF THE DOG: From 7 P.M. to 8:59 P.M.*

DIRECTION OF THIS BRANCH: West-northwest

SEASON AND PRINCIPAL MONTH: Autumn and October

CORRESPONDS TO THE WESTERN SIGN: Libra, the Balance

FIXED ELEMENT: Metal

STEM: Yang, or masculine

* Ascendant: *Children who are born during the two-hour segment of the day ruled by the Dog sign will have this sign as their ascendant and will display affinity for people born under this particular sign, as well as have many of the distinct character traits that identify the Dog sign.*

FIVE CYCLES* OF THE LUNAR YEARS OF THE DOG IN THE WESTERN CALENDAR

START DATE		END DATE	ELEMENT OF THE YEAR
February 6, 1970	to	January 26, 1971	Metal
January 25, 1982	to	February 12, 1983	Water
February 10, 1994	to	January 30, 1995	Wood
January 29, 2006	to	February 17, 2007	Fire
February 16, 2018	to	February 4, 2019	Earth

* A cycle on the lunar horoscope equals twelve years. Five cycles completes sixty years.

Note: One who is born on the day before the start of the lunar year of the Dog, e.g., February 9, 1994, will belong to the animal sign before the Dog, which is the Rooster sign, the tenth lunar sign. One who is born on the day after the end of the lunar year of the Dog, e.g., January 31, 1995, belongs to the animal sign following the Dog, which is the Boar, the twelfth lunar sign.

狗

榮須奮爭 譽不可失

克昌題

美秀畫

THE DOG SIGN

JUST AS FAME MUST BE WON, HONOR MUST NOT BE LOST

The Dog Personality

The eleventh earth branch of the Chinese lunar cycle is named *Xu* and affectionately known as the sign of the Dog. The *Xu* sign symbolizes loyalty and devotion to duty, and likewise a child born in its year will display the same characteristics. The Dog personality will display a sense of purpose and need to protect those he loves early in his life. He tends to be docile and friendly on the outside yet watchful and somewhat restless on the inside. At heart, the Dog personality is a traditional and somewhat suspicious soul and will not give his trust too quickly. Yet once he does warm up, he will give his wholehearted support and loyalty to his friends and family without any reservations. Responsive and pure hearted, the Dog has no problem choosing sides. In his mind, he always picks the winning side. Yes, he is pretty dogmatic when he thinks he is right, and he will be an instinctive fighter who does not back down when he goes on the attack.

A child born under the Dog sign is usually sunny and optimistic in disposition but will have a strong, quick temper when stirred. His primary purpose is to look out for the welfare of others, often neglecting his own interests in the bargain. Unselfish, gallant, and honest, the Dog is not very materialistic or calculating. He is conscientious and has quick reflexes, which may make him good at sports. The native of the *Xu* branch is an excellent team player and understands the need for cooperation and teamwork early in life. He is sometimes too honest and forthright for his own good and is a poor liar. The Dog child just hates to pretend to like someone or something that he does not and will have a sharp tongue and biting comments to show his true feelings. But no matter how tough he may appear, the likeable Dog often has a good sense of humor and can forgive easily.

This child will appreciate the difference between right and wrong early in life and will always be ruled by his conscience. When he hurts someone, he will try to make it up to that person in more ways than one and apologize sincerely. He is able to make strong commitments and hates to let others down, especially his parents and siblings. He always has to justify his actions or the actions of those close to him to see if there is a clear purpose and no ulterior motives under the surface. In times of crisis or distress, he is very self-assured and will stand resolutely like a pillar of strength. The Dog is always guided by a definite sense of belonging, a duty to be fulfilled, a friend to rescue or protect, a cause to champion. He questions his own worthiness and can be a bit spartan in disciplining himself. Most importantly, he is fulfilled when he is able to excel in his duties and responsibilities and serve those he cares about. The modest Dog generates enough self-esteem of his own to never need false praise from others. He is not competitive and cannot be intimidated easily. His straightforward nature and integrity helps him to build strong and useful alliances. He could work alone or with others and has no problem following the lead of a strong mentor. He needs direction and challenges to direct his immense energies and need for close relationships. The levelheaded Dog child is easily inspired by idealism and compassion and looks upon good mentors and parents to guide and love him.

Birth Order and Sibling Rivalry

*FIRSTBORN OR ONLY CHILD

The firstborn Dog child is naturally going to be a top Dog and he will not relinquish his position in this hierarchy. He will be a good leader, as he tends to be reasonable and a good listener. On the negative side, he has a quick temper and will not suffer fools or insubordination. The Dog child in this position will be devoted to his parents and look up to them as his role models in life. Unselfish and democratic in his views, he will be easy to obey, as he is basically obedient and hardworking himself. Although he may be responsible and realistic, this child tends to have a pessimistic and anxious side to his nature when his security or that of his family is threatened. Kind and sociable, he is

* When a child is born five years after another child, he or she is also considered a firstborn child.

able to help his siblings, even when he feels they are undeserving, because of his inborn devotion to duty and need to protect. In school, he will run with the pack and is able to take care of himself from day one.

MIDDLE OR LATER-BORN CHILD

When the Dog child occupies this secondary position, he is less serious and more playful and adventurous. After all, he is not in the top position and there is less expected of him. The pressure to set a good example or to outshine the firstborn is not upon this middle or later-born child, so he is able to develop and advance his own values at a more moderate speed. By nature, he may not be as competitive as the firstborn and is willing to coexist peacefully so long as he is not bullied. This is a laid-back position for the Dog, who really likes to lie by the fireplace or the TV and feel contentment with his family. However, if he is challenged and feels intimidated, he could turn into a staunch defender and unreasonable foe. Loving and kind to the younger siblings, he will overlook their faults and protect them regardless of whether they want his guardianship. He is not as lenient with the older siblings or the firstborn, as he feels they should take care of themselves.

YOUNGEST OR LAST-BORN CHILD

Everyone understands why puppies are universally loved and adored. The Dog born in this position is bound to be most affectionate and charming. He will be known for his levelheaded and sensible approach, and although he may be spoiled, he is not selfish and will love to share whatever he has with his siblings or friends. Parents are more relaxed and experienced by the time the last child arrives and will allow this particular child more freedom and less responsibility. The Dog child in this position expects to tag along with everyone, but will also demand respect as a valued member of the team. If he feels taken for granted or looked down upon, he could be rebellious and cynical in his outlook. On the whole, he loves to please and will be people and progress oriented if he is able to build strong relationships and bonds while he is young and impressionable.

Ascendants

In Chinese horoscopes, the two-hour segment ruling the time of birth is known as the ascendant sign. This can also be referred to as the child's "inner self."

The time of birth used to determine the ascendant is always the local time in the place of birth.

For a child born in the Year of the Dog:

THE RAT ASCENDANT—TIME OF BIRTH IS BETWEEN 11 P.M. AND 12:59 A.M.
With his Rat ascendant, this child attracts others with kindness and a sunny disposition, but has a keen sense of whom to trust with his generosity. The Rat inner self in this Dog child is ever self-preserving as well as a strong protector of the family. He may have a tendency to be oversensitive or overprotective when anything threatens his interests or the family's. Fortunately, this child assesses character almost flawlessly and makes good judgments accordingly. However, the crafty Rat makes this Dog personality more calculating, and as a result, he is able to look out for his own interests and finances. An eloquent speaker and critic of those whom he finds lacking in fair play and morality, this little Dog has a big voice and a sharp tongue to match.

THE OX ASCENDANT—TIME OF BIRTH IS BETWEEN 1 A.M. AND 2:59 A.M.
Sincere honesty influences this child's birth hour with the strong Ox as his ascendant. He will take a dedicated interested in hobbies and labor over them calmly and diligently. No surprise this patient Dog child will be a model student and citizen. The only area where he could improve is in that of taking risks and going out on a limb. The traditional Ox as his inner self will want this Dog personality to travel the straight and narrow path. His Dog nature will value truth and integrity to a fault, and he will be happiest when he is able to help others. A loving child and true friend to the end, this Dog native will find his calling in doing volunteer or missionary work, where his greatest reward will be knowing that he makes a difference in the lives of others.

THE TIGER ASCENDANT—TIME OF BIRTH IS BETWEEN 3 A.M. AND 4:59 A.M.

With the remarkable Tiger as his inner self, this child will be extremely driven toward his dreams, no matter how lofty. The ambitious Tiger and the loyal Dog both possess a great deal of energy and determination and are often guided by high ideals. The Tiger ascendant here could be controversial and tends to be temperamental and volatile. The Dog does not fear new challenges and is not intimidated easily, so this Dog child may gravitate toward the stage lights or be a high-profile performer of the theatre or even politics. Though, at times, this combination has a tendency toward being a tireless activist, a healthy balance can be found with age and good parenting. This Dog personality possesses true sincerity and is a champion of the less fortunate.

THE RABBIT ASCENDANT—TIME OF BIRTH IS BETWEEN 5 A.M. AND 6:59 A.M.

The diplomatic Rabbit ascendant may create a Dog who is careful to weigh all options and is able to hold his tongue. The gentle Rabbit provides more decorum to the otherwise boisterous Dog, who does not run at the first sign of trouble but may even welcome a battle or two. The Rabbit as the inner self looks for peaceful and sensible ways to avoid trouble and may influence the idealistic Dog to take the middle of the road when he is not able to have his way. With a "live to fight another day" attitude, this Dog is practical and able to bide his time well. Soft-spoken but knowledgeable, this particular Dog child will not give his trust or opinion easily to strangers and is reserved in making quick judgments. He will have excellent people skills and can tell friend from foe instinctively.

THE DRAGON ASCENDANT—TIME OF BIRTH IS BETWEEN 7 A.M. AND 8:59 A.M.

The powerful Dragon ascendant could produce an idealistic Dog who believes in miracles. He may even turn out to be a miracle worker, with his tireless devotion to truth and beauty. The Dog nature does not hunger for power but will diligently preserve and protect what is his. The Dragon as the inner self is more goal oriented and needs power in order to cement his leadership. Hopefully, this child will be able to fulfill his dreams by using both his Dog instincts and his Dragon inclinations. He is not above being very tough with anyone who breaks the rules. And, quite often, he will be the one who sets the rules. He is a great friend but a dangerous enemy. The Dragon ascendant makes this Dog less of a team player and more of a visionary leader.

THE SNAKE ASCENDANT—TIME OF BIRTH IS BETWEEN 9 A.M. AND 10:59 A.M.

This Dog child will be more of an intellectual with the enigmatic Snake ascendant. Quiet, competent, and self-possessed, a Dog child with this inner self is bound to be more egoistic and secretive. The Snake is tenacious and approaches his goals with great purpose, while the Dog tends to care more about others than himself. This is a good combination if this Dog personality uses his wisdom and energy for the common good instead of selfish gains. On the surface, he can be calm and friendly, yet he is not above plotting and suspicions when he feels threatened or insecure. This is a watchful and diligent Dog child who is able to size up situations and knows his own strengths and weaknesses. He is faithful and persevering, but can be vindictive and unforgiving when he is hurt or cheated.

THE HORSE ASCENDANT—TIME OF BIRTH IS BETWEEN 11 A.M. AND 12:59 P.M.

When the steadfast Dog is born during the hours of the Horse, he will have a sunny and happy disposition and a rather adventurous view of life. He is very sportive and wants constant activity and excitement to liven up things. Gifted with good intuition and a keen sense of fair play, this Dog youngster is observant, easy to please, and cooperative. His one drawback may be his impatience and short attention span, because his Horse inner self loves to do several things at one time and sees the grass as greener on the other side. He will have many friends because he will be loyal and will defend them against all odds. At home, he will try his best to get along with everyone and has an even temper, with the exception of the occasional outburst when he is frustrated or left out of some activity.

THE SHEEP ASCENDANT—TIME OF BIRTH IS BETWEEN 1 P.M. AND 2:59 P.M.

The Sheep ascendant makes this Dog child more sensitive and creative than others of the same sign. With this warm and kindhearted inner self, this Dog child is generous and understanding. He cares deeply about his family and will nurture others with his sincere desire to be helpful and sympathetic. Yet the watchful Dog combined with the often indulgent Sheep personality could also be a chronic complainer who needs to sound off and get the attention he craves. However, he does have many supporters and close friends who appreciate his soft-hearted nature and know that he will be there for them in times of trouble. People will open their hearts and minds to this outgoing personality. This is a good mix of contrast between the egalitarian Dog and the compassionate but sometimes inconsistent Sheep personality. He will be drawn to team activity and contact sports.

THE MONKEY ASCENDANT—TIME OF BIRTH IS BETWEEN 3 P.M. AND 4:59 P.M.

With the Monkey as his ascendant, this Dog is witty and quite an imaginative little imp when he wants to be. A good negotiator and shrewd manipulator of his parents, he knows how to present his case very convincingly and will be a master of strategy. With the Dog's keen sense of duty and accountability and the ingenious Monkey's curiosity and enthusiasm for solving difficult problems, this child will be much sought after for his practical ability and good sense. Versatile and clever, he is outspoken and realistic and can handle his own affairs well. A capable student who is goal oriented, this child possesses a great sense of humor and positive outlook that will make him a winner wherever he goes. The Dog personality is able to protect what is his, while the Monkey as his inner self is always on the lookout for new and better opportunities. Others will be smart to follow his lead.

THE ROOSTER ASCENDANT—TIME OF BIRTH IS BETWEEN 5 P.M. AND 6:59 P.M.

The colorful Rooster as this Dog's ascendant makes him opinionated and analytical in his views. The Dog loves balance and strives for equality. The Rooster could be controversial and picky because he is really a perfectionist at heart and cannot stand idleness. In this special combination, each half should work at being less rigid. Thankfully, the Dog part is more cooperative and flexible, while the Rooster may be domineering and critical. Both signs are dutiful and industrious, with the Rooster as the studious and knowledgeable driving force. This brave Dog child definitely has the formula for success if he follows his own intuition yet also uses his Rooster diligence and attention to details. This is a not too generous Dog personality who keeps a sharp eye on the accounts and sticks to his budget.

THE DOG ASCENDANT—TIME OF BIRTH IS BETWEEN 7 P.M. AND 8:59 P.M.

This is an alert and defensive Dog doing double duty with the same ascendant as his birth sign. He is definitely likeable but could be a chronic worrier as he sets out to defend the world from injustice like a Ralph Nader disciple. It would be hard to fault his sincerity and honesty, as he works tirelessly to warn and protect his home and loved ones. No matter how docile and amiable he may appear at times, his bite is as bad as his bark. He has a big heart and can be generous and selfless in his devotion. But at times he could also be the ultimate revolutionary when he finds a cause to champion or a wrong to right. He has great faith in himself and will follow his heart and convictions. However, this child is people oriented and works well with others who have the same level of commitment that he has. He can be depended on to stand his ground and be observant and loyal. He is the Warrior Dog.

THE BOAR ASCENDANT—TIME OF BIRTH IS BETWEEN 9 P.M. AND 10:59 P.M.

With the passionate Boar ruling his birth hour, this happy-go-lucky Dog child will find great pleasure in the finer things life has to offer. Yes, he will still stand guard and care about the welfare of others, but this doesn't mean he can't live a little. Sociable, charismatic, and fearless, this Dog personality can be relentless when he sets his heart and mind on something he desires. Blessed with a big heart and a wonderful capacity to love and bond with others, there is little this

Dog child will not do for his family and close friends. As a result, others do take advantage of his largesse and kind nature. He can be emotionally charged when challenged, but he has the strength of character to take his responsibilities seriously.

Famous Persons Born in the Year of the Dog

Mother Teresa

Sir Winston Churchill

Andre Agassi

Boutros Boutros Ghali

Elvis Presley

Ralph Nader

Sophia Loren

King Gustav of Sweden

Victor Hugo

Donald Trump

Itzhak Rabin

Pierre Cardin

Carl Sagan

Prince William

Zhou Enlai

Voltaire

Judy Garland

Herbert Hoover

Claude Debussy

King Albert of Belgium

Brigitte Bardot

Carol Burnett

Cher

William J. Clinton

Madonna

Charles Bronson

Ava Gardner

Norman Mailer

Golda Meir

Robert Louis Stevenson

As a treat to your child, please read the Dog's story,
"How the Guardian Dogs Saved Their Village," which follows.

THE DOG'S STORY

"HOW THE GUARDIAN DOGS SAVED THEIR VILLAGE"

Since the beginning of time, the celestial hound ran alongside Erh Lang, the fearsome immortal who acted as the chief law enforcer of the heavenly rulers. All Dogs were said to have descended from Erh Lang's celestial hound that now lives in the Dog Star in the heavens.

This story is about two lion Dogs who lived in a village high in the Tibetan mountains. The male Dog was large and fearful looking with bulging eyes, but was actually very gentle and shy. His name was Bao, which means "precious" or "treasure." The female lion Dog was named Mei, which means "pretty" in Chinese, and she was pretty. Like her mate, Mei's coat looked like a giant flower with its tricolored curly fur. No one was quite sure of when they arrived in the village or where these two Dogs came from. But it was a belief in Tibet that the arrival of a Dog meant good fortune and prosperity, so the two Dogs were welcomed with open arms in the village. They were affectionately called Bao-Bao and Mei-Mei, in the same way that the Chinese repeat the names of young children.

Bao-Bao and Mei-Mei took up residence in the old temple that faced the entrance of the village square. And since they sort of belonged to everyone yet no one in particular, everyone brought food and water to the Dogs. The Dogs were well taken care of and they lived a carefree and happy life as part of the entire village family. Eventually, they had a pup and would allow the children to play with their pup.

Occasionally, the Dogs would bark at the arrival of a stranger or merchants from out of town. But most of the time, they were peaceful and docile and got along well with the other animals, especially the horses and donkeys. Then, one day, Bao-Bao noticed a change in the atmosphere of the village and sensed that it came from the tall mountain that rose up in front of the village. Bao-Bao and

Mei-Mei sensed an evil presence in the mountains and started to bark to convey their fear to their friends the villagers.

Of course, no one understood why the Dogs were barking so much, let alone appreciated the angry and urgent tone of the Dogs' bark. Bao-Bao and Mei-Mei became restless and watchful and could not stop barking. They also tried to prevent anyone from leaving the village to go up the mountain. One morning, as a woodcutter was walking up the mountain, the two Dogs tried to pull him back by biting his sleeves and tugging at his trousers. The woodcutter screamed at them and struck them with his walking stick.

That evening, the woodcutter did not return to the village. The next morning, his family and a group of men went up the mountain to search for him and found him sleeping under a gigantic tree. However, when they tried to wake him, they realized that the woodcutter was dead. Bao-Bao and Mei-Mei barked furiously when they came back with the woodcutter's body, their fur stood on end, and their eyes became red and angry. Now the villagers began to understand why the Dogs were behaving so strangely.

"The Dogs sensed danger and evil and we did not heed their warning," said a wise elder of the village.

"But what kind of danger could it be? There are no marks on the woodcutter's body, nor any sign of a struggle," said a puzzled relative of the dead man.

Yet, after the mysterious death of the woodcutter, animals became sick and the chickens stopped laying eggs. Then another man who went up into the mountain was found dead, under the same tree as the woodcutter was. He, too, looked like he was just sleeping.

This time, the herbalist named Ling, who served as the only doctor in town, decided to take a closer look at the body and discovered tiny marks around the eyes of the dead man. When he looked into the mouth of the dead person, he saw that his tongue was green.

"What a disturbing and strange malady," observed the herbalist. "We must not venture into the mountain until we know more."

However, a week later, another man went up into the mountain for firewood and the same thing happened. By now, the two Dogs stationed themselves at the entrance of the village and stared up at the gigantic tree in the mountain. They ate little and did not sleep much. When the wind blew down from the mountain, Bao-Bao and Mei-Mei's fur would stand on end and they would bark until they were hoarse. No one knew what to make of this terrible situation, until the herbalist suggested that the Dogs could perhaps see what human eyes could not.

"The Dogs have seen an invisible enemy up in the giant tree. This invisible enemy must be responsible for the sleeping deaths of the three men. The only reason the invisible enemy has not yet invaded our village is because it is afraid of Bao-Bao and Mei-Mei. There can be no other explanation," observed the wise herbalist.

"How can we fight an invisible enemy?" asked the frightened villagers.

"If only the Dogs can see the invisible enemy, then only the Dogs can defeat it," came the answer.

By now, the two Dogs were exhausted from barking and growling and looked nothing like their former happy selves. They were shedding clumps of fur from their beautiful thick coats. Then, one day, quite by accident, one of the mothers took some of the Dogs' fur, rolled it up into a ball, and put it in a little cloth bag, which she then hung around her child's neck for protection against the unknown evil. More mothers did the same thing and were glad that their children did not get sick anymore, and those who were sick got well.

However, the villagers still dared not go up the mountain to cut wood and did not venture out after dark. They were all afraid and would not allow their children to even go out and play in the yard. Life became quite miserable, since everyone felt as if they were being watched by an unseen presence high up in the gigantic tree on the mountains. One night when the moon was full, the two lion Dogs disappeared and did not return the next morning. The awful silence of their absence overwhelmed the tiny village. No one knew what to do next. They even missed the loud, incessant barking and growling of Bao-Bao and Mei-Mei, which usually frightened them.

Finally, on the third day, the villagers summoned up their courage to go and look for the two Dogs in the light of day. They headed for the giant tree where they had found all the three victims of the sleeping death. There in the clearing under the massive tree lay Bao-Bao and Mei-Mei with their teeth gripped on a large, scaly creature that looked like a lizard. It had two heads and the Dogs apparently each bit one head and hung on until it died. But in their battle to destroy the creature, both Dogs gave their lives.

"Now, only after it is dead, can we see the invisible enemy as the Dogs did. This is the evil that came to dwell in this gigantic tree, and we are fortunate that the Dogs could see it for what it really was," said one of the monks.

The villagers burned the evil creature and buried it under the tree. They took the Dogs' bodies home and gave them a proper funeral with incense and all the traditional ceremonies. But still they mourned the loss of such loyal friends. So they decided to carve stone statues in the likeness of the two lion Dogs and placed them respectfully in front of the temple gates, where they loved to be.

Bao-Bao is shown as his playful yet serious self with a ball under one paw, and Mei-Mei's statue shows her lovingly protecting her pup between her paws. Since that time, every household and temple and even royal palaces around China have statues of this pair of famous lion Dogs, guarding their entryways and keeping watch for any kind of evil, seen or unseen.

CHAPTER TWELVE

THE BOAR

The Twelfth Lunar Sign

The Boar child is treasured for

Her goodwill and universal fellowship.

Pure of heart, this sign is

Blessed with strength and purity.

She possesses great fortitude

And a zest for life.

By giving freely of herself,

She is richer and reaps more benefits.

Chivalrous, open, and approachable,

The Boar personality is lavish with affection

As well as with her money.

Above all, she loves to bring people together.

She is admired as the unifier of the cycle.

Her motto is: **A GOOD HEART BRINGS A GOOD REWARD!**

CHINESE NAME FOR THE BOAR: *Zhu*

RANK: Twelfth

HOURS OF THE BOAR: From 9 P.M. to 10:59 P.M.*

DIRECTION OF THIS BRANCH: North-northwest

SEASON AND PRINCIPAL MONTH: Autumn and November

CORRESPONDS TO THE WESTERN SIGN: Scorpio, the Scorpion

FIXED ELEMENT: Water

STEM: Yin, or feminine

188

T
H
E

B
O
A
R

* Ascendant: *Children who are born during the two-hour segment of the day ruled by the Boar sign will have this sign as their ascendant and will display affinity for people born under this particular sign, as well as have many of the distinct character traits that identify the Boar sign.*

FIVE CYCLES* OF THE LUNAR YEARS OF THE BOAR IN THE WESTERN CALENDAR

START DATE		END DATE	ELEMENT OF THE YEAR
January 27, 1971	to	January 15, 1972	Metal
February 13, 1983	to	February 1, 1984	Water
January 31, 1995	to	February 18, 1996	Wood
February 18, 2007	to	February 6, 2008	Fire
February 5, 2019	to	January 24, 2020	Earth

* A cycle on the lunar horoscope equals twelve years. Five cycles completes sixty years.

Note: One who is born on the day before the start of the lunar year of the Boar, e.g., January 30, 1995, will belong to the animal sign before the Boar, which is the Dog sign, the eleventh lunar sign. One who is born on the day after the end of the lunar year of the Boar, e.g., February 19, 1996, belongs to the animal sign following the Boar, which is the Rat, the first lunar sign.

THE BOAR SIGN

A GOOD HEART BRINGS A GOOD REWARD

The Boar Personality

The twelfth earth branch of the Chinese lunar cycle is called *Hai* and its animal sign is the Boar, or the Pig. Because the Pig is a domesticated version, I have chosen to call the natives of the *Hai* branch Boars, to show their true passionate and intense natures. A child born under the *Hai* branch is an optimist with a huge supply of energy. Everyone who comes in contact with her is affected by her vitality and warmth. Never halfhearted about anything, she always has a contribution to make. This vivacious and enthusiastic child of the twelfth earth branch could be a joyous bundle of love, sparkling with vigor.

Part social worker, part evangelist, one hundred percent commitment to push her convictions through is usually this child's goal. Her dedication is dictated by the strength of motivation she feels. If she is not motivated or inspired, it will be difficult just to get her out of bed each morning. But once she believes in something and wants it bad enough, it will be hard to suppress her total devotion and gregarious and grand-scale inclinations. And throughout history, Boars have become captains of industries and built huge fortunes or improved the lives of the masses by their far-reaching business acumen and foresight.

The Boar can be assertive and endearing at the same time. Her powers of persuasion are unique and inspiring. She will have an excellent capacity for organizing group efforts and large-scale functions where everyone and everything will have to come together smoothly. Her intelligence and people skills are inborn, and Boars naturally are voted as most popular or most likely to succeed wherever they go. Likewise, they have no fear about being chosen to head the class or be in charge of the committee to raise funds or gather up a million signatures. They really believe they can do the impossible, and usually they succeed with the overwhelming support of family and friends.

The Boar child is very giving and willing to sacrifice herself and to contribute whatever she can for the good of others. When the Boar personality is focused and directs her many talents where they are needed, her leadership is incomparable. When she is left to her own devices and drifts from one project to another without the proper guidance and support, she can be easily depressed and will let everything go. A good way to know if the Boar is happy is to watch her weight. When she is frustrated, she will overindulge and put on weight. But when she snaps out of her down moods or falls in love, she will immediately lose weight and have a whole new and positive outlook. Good at public relations and rallying people, the Boar is never at a loss for ways to drum up support. She is a great fund-raiser at sport events and any charity that piques her interest. Spontaneous in her actions, the Boar is very easy to love and appreciate because of her generosity and openness. However, she is naive in her faith in others and must learn at an early age how to avoid being taken advantage of and being used by others with selfish motives. Unfortunately, there are few shortcuts in life and the chivalrous and good-hearted Boar may have to learn many painful lessons the hard way before she becomes more cautious and restrained. But the Boar may not want it any other way. At heart, she is the ultimate humanitarian and she will always believe in the goodness of humankind.

Birth Order and Sibling Rivalry

*FIRSTBORN OR ONLY CHILD

A Boar in this birth position will be a positive influence on her family. She is unselfish and helpful and feels that there is plenty of love and food to go around. She enjoys the camaraderie of siblings, and if she is an only child, she will have a large circle of friends, most of them gathering at the Boar's home for all sorts of club meetings and get-togethers. This Boar will also have a tendency to be a big spender and will expect her parents to fund her many social events. Younger siblings will look up to her, as she will truly love them and can deny her family nothing. She loves the responsibility of caring for others and being in charge.

* When a child is born five years after another child, he or she is also considered a firstborn child.

MIDDLE OR LATER-BORN CHILD

A Boar child in this position can be a bit thick-skinned, competitive, and brash. She has to be. She feels she needs to show that she can and should take up a big load for her parents and may resent it if she feels the firstborn is not doing enough. Reliable and good at making friends, this Boar is proud and passionate in her loyalties, but at times she does not exert enough control over her life because she wants to do everything and be everywhere. Working hard to make herself indispensable, she finds it difficult to be detached in her affections and to curtail her commitments. However, she always has a positive frame of mind and will treat setbacks like water coming off a duck's back.

YOUNGEST OR LAST-BORN CHILD

As the youngest or last-born child, the Boar is very happy to be the baby of the family. Here, she is able to be competitive and outgoing, but she won't have the stress and pressure that come from parents' having too many expectations. Although this Boar may be the most naive of the bunch, she has great faith in herself and will set out to accomplish whatever she sets her mind to with such gusto and exuberance that others will bet on her succeeding. She doesn't take no for an answer, and with her energetic and persuasive personality, she will be able to gather people from different walks of life or even opposing points of view to unite under her courageous leadership. Demonstrative and affectionate, this Boar has a good nature and a knack for uniting people.

Ascendants

In Chinese horoscopes, the two-hour segment ruling the time of birth is known as the ascendant sign. This can also be referred to as the child's "inner self."

The time of birth used to determine the ascendant is always the local time in the place of birth.

For a child born in the Year of the Boar:

THE RAT ASCENDANT—TIME OF BIRTH IS BETWEEN 11 P.M. AND 12:59 A.M.

With the Rat as her ascendant, this Boar child could be carefree yet crafty and enjoys social success by being popular, but she is not a pushover to be taken advantage of. The Rat is calculating and as the inner self should protect the Boar against her own naivete. The Boar personality is naturally tough and resilient and is not complicated or conniving. With the Rat as her inner self here, she will no doubt be even more loving and devoted to family and may be indulgent in satisfying her own desires. This is a good combination of fortitude and astute intelligence. This Boar child could also thank the Rat for her sharp tongue and ability to avoid trouble, not to mention saving up for that rainy day.

THE OX ASCENDANT—TIME OF BIRTH IS BETWEEN 1 A.M. AND 2:59 A.M.

When the trusting Boar is blessed with the Ox ascendant, she feels more secure and stable. The Ox is disciplined and will adhere to strict rules, forcing the Boar half to curb her excesses and face reality. With the Ox as her inner self, this normally congenial and easygoing Boar will set high standards and have strong likes and dislikes. People won't be able to push her around so easily or ask her for favors or even loans. The serious outlook of the Ox ascendant makes this Boar child able to resist temptations and be more selective in making commitments. She won't be as generous as other Boars and will have a certain individualism that others respect. She is a strong and able personality who plans and organizes with a budget that is workable.

THE TIGER ASCENDANT—TIME OF BIRTH IS BETWEEN 3 A.M. AND 4:59 A.M.

Here is a big-hearted and dazzling Boar with the Tiger as her inner self. This particular ascendant gives this Boar child more passion and color than she already has. The extroverted Tiger has a zest for life equal to the sensual Boar. With this dynamic alter ego, this Boar child is captivating and led by her powerful emotions. She will not want to take the middle of the road and everything she does will be dramatic and noteworthy. A natural for the stage and theatre, she will exploit her many talents and be a real showperson. A commanding performer, this Boar-Tiger combination will shine as an entertainer or organizer and be much sought after for her excellent skills at making things happen.

THE RABBIT ASCENDANT—TIME OF BIRTH IS BETWEEN 5 A.M. AND 6:59 A.M.

With the debonair Rabbit ascendant, this Boar child will definitely not want to carry anything more than her load of any burden. She will skillfully defer responsibility and will not care to be imposed upon or make too many sacrifices. The Rabbit is prudent and practical and will advise the Boar half to look after her own interests. As a result, this Boar is less trusting of others and will not be as obliging as other Boars. With the Rabbit as her inner self, this particular Boar will be more intuitive and discerning. She will be tactful and careful in her actions and hopefully look before she leaps or make commitments. This Boar-Rabbit combination is not as generous or outgoing as other Boars, but still she does enjoy giving a party, especially if she can get someone else to pay for it.

THE DRAGON ASCENDANT—TIME OF BIRTH IS BETWEEN 7 A.M. AND 8:59 A.M.

Having the mighty Dragon as her ascendant makes this Boar a chivalrous and dedicated person. Strong and benevolent, this Boar likes to take on huge responsibilities and is happiest when she can get everyone involved in a worthy project. Yet both signs here are trusting and innocent in their purity of mind and heart and will need shrewd partners and supporters to look out for them. Without capable advisers and accountants, this particular Boar may get carried away by her optimism and excesses. However, the Dragon inner self provides the leadership and respect that the Boar half needs to achieve her dreams. This is an energetic combination because both signs enjoy hard work, duty, social functions, and sports.

THE SNAKE ASCENDANT—TIME OF BIRTH IS BETWEEN 9 A.M. AND 10:59 A.M.

The intellectual and introverted Snake ascendant makes this Boar calm and collected. She pursues her objectives with intensity and consistency. With the

Snake as her inner self, this Boar is not trusting at all but looks to herself for acquiring knowledge and power. This Boar could be vindictive and unforgiving if she is ever cheated or hurt, and she tends to keep her feelings inside. She takes rejection hard but does not give up easily. These two signs have opposite inclinations, so this particular child will be complicated and difficult to read at times. She knows how to bide her time and will not want to do anything in which she does not understand her benefits or advantages. This is a forceful Boar with deep emotions, large appetites, and long-term planning abilities.

THE HORSE ASCENDANT—TIME OF BIRTH IS BETWEEN 11 A.M. AND 12:59 P.M.

The confident and adventurous Horse ascendant here brings this Boar a joyous approach to life. However, both signs here may be impulsive and strong-willed, and this child will be accustomed to having her own way. The Horse half is direct and more self-centered than the self-sacrificing Boar half. With the Horse as her inner self, this Boar is charming, but quick to bolt if too much is asked of her. She is a quick-witted personality who will be recognized for her intelligence and flexibility. The Horse will most likely make away with the Boar's scruples and need for approval. Here the Horse ascendant gives the Boar personality more independence and self-reliance than normal.

THE SHEEP ASCENDANT—TIME OF BIRTH IS BETWEEN 1 P.M. AND 2:59 P.M.

The compassion and refinement of the Sheep ascendant enhances the generous qualities of the trusting Boar. Hopefully, this peaceful and artistic personality will find many supporters and mentors who will protect and guide her. Her one big problem is not being able to deny herself anything, with a tendency to indulge herself and her friends in the finer things in life. Yet she will be always cared for and rewarded for her caring and sympathetic ways. She is always ready to help out and willing to lend an ear in times of trouble. This loving Boar-Sheep personality is not judgmental and can accept others for what they are. Consequently, she is always able to find people who will be willing to work with her or help her.

THE MONKEY ASCENDANT—TIME OF BIRTH IS BETWEEN 3 P.M. AND 4:59 P.M.

The Monkey ascendant will guard the Boar against being tricked or taken advantage of. Clever and self-assured, this Boar child will be able to fend for herself and will know how to make the best of any bargain with the Monkey as her inner self. Inventive and ambitious, the Boar is charitable but only if she also benefits from all her good deeds. The Monkey half will see to that. Here the sociable qualities of the helpful Boar will be merged with the keen capability of the Monkey to seek out good deals. Both signs in this combination are affectionate and lively. The Boar loves life and will be indulgent and sensuous in pursuing her many appetites and interests. The clever Monkey half may be successful in curbing the spending of the Boar and teaching her new ways to manipulate things to her advantage while saving some bucks.

THE ROOSTER ASCENDANT—TIME OF BIRTH IS BETWEEN 5 P.M. AND 6:59 P.M.

With the Rooster as her ascendant here, this Boar child will be studious and meticulous in her approach to life. The eccentric Rooster may bring order and frugality into this happy and outgoing Boar personality. Full of good intentions and advice, this unique combination could have eccentric ways of doing things and controlling others. The Rooster half can be critical, whereas the Boar is laid back and easygoing. If the Rooster part is holding the purse strings, the indulgent Boar may not like to spend unless she gets good value for her money. The efficient and resourceful Rooster part in this combination may finally get the Boar half to realize her true worth.

THE DOG ASCENDANT—TIME OF BIRTH IS BETWEEN 7 P.M. AND 8:59 P.M.

With the sensible and practical Dog ascendant as her ally, this Boar is direct and bold. Fearless and brave in helping others, this Boar-Dog combination is fair-minded and will not be afraid to give her opinion or stick by her convictions. This is an unselfish combination who looks out for the welfare of her family and loved ones. She is willing to make great sacrifices to protect others and may neglect her own interests in her zeal to right wrongs and follow her ideals. Yet

the Boar is always lucky in finding supporters, and with the Dog's honesty and integrity, this combination should have no problem coming out ahead. The Dog half is not as trusting or giving as the naive Boar, which is really a blessing in disguise for this Boar.

THE BOAR ASCENDANT—TIME OF BIRTH IS BETWEEN 9 P.M. AND 10:59 P.M.

A double Boar personality brings great fortitude and strength to this child. However, all the positive and negative qualities are also increased. This personality is very intense and magnanimous. She knows no limits when she is intent on achieving her goal and will be able to tolerate any suffering or carry any burden to reach success. She puts her heart and soul into everything she does and will attract many friends and supporters by her irrepressible energy and imposing and contagious optimism. Here again, this particular Boar personality could have huge appetites and excesses and be fatalistic in her desires and ambitions. She goes for the "all or nothing" slogan and is especially hard on herself, while giving her friends and loved ones the benefit of the doubt.

197

ASCENDANTS

Famous Persons Born in the Year of the Boar

Henry Ford
Ronald Reagan
Steven Spielberg
Merle Oberon
Glenn Close
Prince Rainier of Monaco
Henry Kissinger
The Dalai Lama
Andrew Jackson
Francoise Sagan
King Hussein
Ernest Hemingway
Alfred Hitchcock
Duchess of York
Luciano Pavarotti
Arnold Schwarzenegger
King Henry VIII

Jose Carreras
Hubert Humphrey
Lucille Ball
Prince Bernhard of the Netherlands
Sir Noel Coward
Maria Callas
Field Marshal Montgomery
Chiang Kai-Shek
Hillary Rodham Clinton
Ralph Waldo Emerson
Julie Andrews
Tracey Ullman
Humphrey Bogart
John D. Rockefeller
Woody Allen
Elton John

198

T
H
E

B
O
A
R

As a treat to your child, please read the Boar's story,
"How the Boars Moved a Mountain," which follows.

THE BOAR'S STORY

"HOW THE BOARS MOVED A MOUNTAIN"

A very long time ago, when the world was just beginning and animals could talk with each other and when humans knew how to listen, there lived a wonderful family of Boars. The Boar clan lived peacefully in a large collection of caves under one of the Twin Mountains. These Twin Mountains lay in the eastern part of the Middle Kingdom where the sun first rises each day; it was a beautiful and tranquil place. The Boar clan ate roots and all sorts of vegetation in the deep woods surrounding their massive caves, which had many entrances and exits.

Not too far away from the Twin Mountains, on a majestic hill surrounded by a lake, lived the young emperor in his summer palace. The emperor and his people were kind to the animals and would travel through the long and narrow pass between the two mountains at the onset of each winter so that they could stay in the Winter Palace, which was closer to the southern end of his empire. When the lake froze, it meant that all the important occupants were gone from the Summer Palace and only a few guards and caretakers were left to look after the place.

This story is about the most fascinating and gracious Boar whose name was Duchess. Duchess was a young and outgoing sow who was famous throughout the kingdom as a helpful and generous animal. She always had a good word to say about everyone, and she could communicate well with both animals and humans. Unlike the male Boars of her clan, who preferred to keep to themselves, Duchess had a great number of friends and never turned away anyone who was in need of her aid. Duchess was a tireless worker who organized all sorts of social events and charitable work.

Everyone in the forest had a story to tell about how Duchess had helped them. Mama Goat would recount how Duchess helped her find her baby goat with her keen sense of smell. Duchess also located lost Rabbits and baby deer when they strayed too far from home. Farmer Wu was also grateful to Duchess, who helped him remove a huge tree that had fallen in front of his wagon during a storm. The Boar's strong tusks made it an easy job to lift heavy things and push them out of the way.

Duchess would spend her days helping others forage for food in difficult-to-reach places or would diligently turn over rocks or dig into old tree roots for her most favorite food of all: truffles. Truffles were tasty mushrooms that had a delicious flavor and texture that all Boars loved. Duchess was an expert at finding this delicacy.

Then one summer, discord and trouble seemed to come to the Summer Palace with the hot winds. There was much traffic through the narrow mountain pass and soldiers and guards increased in numbers as the days went by. No brightly lit lanterns and floating barges decorated the placid lake around the palace as in years past. Instead, horses and men galloped urgently in and out of the emperor's home while fierce soldiers stood watch on the ramparts.

A stag who saw what was happening became frightened and asked Duchess, "What does this mean? The humans seem to have become hostile and defensive."

"I don't like it," said the fox, who sniffed the air and shook his head, "smells like trouble to me."

"The only other time I have seen such activity from these humans," said the old bear, "was about three decades ago, and I think they called it a war."

"A war!" cried the others in horror.

"What can that be?" asked an innocent Rabbit who was too young to know the meaning of the word.

"Now, now, dear friends," said Duchess calmly. "Let's not jump to any conclusions and expect the worst. I shall visit Farmer Wu and ask him if he has heard any news of all this activity."

Everyone agreed that Duchess did have a good and sensible approach and felt better with her calm and intelligent behavior. So Duchess went to see Farmer Wu that very same day, and she found him tending his sheep and chickens.

"All this commotion of soldiers riding up and down the mountain is upsetting my animals," complained Farmer Wu to Duchess.

"Do you know what is going on in the palace and why we are having so many soldiers riding about?" asked the worried Duchess.

"Well, I hate to be the one to tell bad news, but it seems some warlord in the West is trying to take over the kingdom and wishes to take our young emperor prisoner. These messengers bring news of how the warlord's army is conquering many other towns and cities and is now approaching the Summer Palace. The emperor dares not leave because he has no safe place to go right now. Ah, such awful politics. It is rumored that even some of the emperor's relatives are spies and may actually work for the enemy," said Farmer Wu sadly.

"Oh, dear," said Duchess. "So it is true. We are going to have a war. How dreadful for the young emperor! I wish we could help."

"What can we do against such powerful forces?" asked Farmer Wu. "We have no armor or weapons or even basic fighting skills. All we can hope for is not to get caught in the middle."

Day by day, Duchess and her friends watched as the conflict grew larger by the numbers of couriers to the palace. They could all sense the fear and growing threat to the emperor, who was now under siege in his summer home. Farmer Wu would inform Duchess of whatever news he heard from other merchants and travelers. Every day, Duchess and her many friends would gather at the top of the mountain to see if there was any sign of the warlord and his army.

Finally, after the summer reached its peak, Duchess and her friends spotted the approaching army slowly winding its way like a serpent toward the Twin Mountains. A frantic Farmer Wu met Duchess and said, "They are coming! All of you must run away and hide! I am taking my family up to the other side of the mountain to find a hidden cave to stay in until these barbarians have gone."

"No, we must stop them before they get here or it will be too late for the emperor," said Duchess bravely.

"Are you out of your minds?" asked Farmer Wu. "What could you simple animals do?"

But Duchess had already left to go back to her clan. Duchess gathered her many brothers and sisters and together they dug up boulders and pushed them down the mountain. They successfully blocked the long narrow pass between Twin Mountains with many huge rocks and boulders so that no could get through. They were quite relieved that their quick action prevented the warlord from approaching the Summer Palace.

However, in a few days, the warlord's army cleared the passage of boulders and widened the road again so that their horses and wagons could enter the gorge. They beat their drums loudly as they started their march, driving fear into all the farmers and peaceful people of the area.

Just when it looked like all was lost, they felt the earth move and shift its weight. Duchess had gotten her whole clan to come out of their caves and line up against the base of the mountain. There was the biggest grandfather Boar with two enormous pairs of tusks that were ten feet long, and uncles who had wide shoulders and bristles that were as thick as armor, along with the rest of the mighty Boars. Duchess stood above them all and shouted:

"Heave! Everybody heave!"

And the mountain slowly moved and merged with its twin. As the passage closed, the warlord and all his men and horses quickly ran out of the way, fleeing for their lives—vowing never to return. They could not understand how a mountain could move and were simply beside themselves with terror, fearing the gods in heaven had moved the mountain to punish them for their evil deeds.

When the young emperor found out how the Boars and especially Duchess had saved him and his kingdom, he granted all the Boars the special military rank of general. It became an emblem of courage and strength for the military to carry a flag with the picture of a charging boar. In China, the nickname for a general became "long-snout warrior." Being called a long-snout warrior was considered a great honor because of the legendary Boars that had the strength and courage to move a mountain.

INDEX

I
N
D
E
X

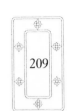

209

211

213